MW00777192

..., by Patti Rose Trueheart

(Under the names Patti Rose or Patti R Rose)

Health Equity, Diversity, and Inclusion: Context, Controversies and Solutions, Second Edition

Health Disparities, Diversity and Inclusion: Context, Controversies, and Solutions, First Edition.

Cultural Competency for the Health Professional

Cultural Competency for Health Administration and Public Health

In Search of Serenity: A Black Family's Struggle with the Threat of AIDS

Cookbook

Effie's Soul Food Recipes and More with a Healthy Twist

Booklets

Forgiveness for Your Student Loans: A Survival Guide Part I

Forgiveness for Your Student Loans: A Survival Guide Part II

Children's Books

Himalia's Dream Venture

Himalia Gets a Dog

Himalia Gets a Passport

A Return to
Black Love

The Joys of Black Fatherhood,

Motherhood, and Marriage Revealed

♥

Black Love is The Answer...

Patti Rose Trueheart

Patti Rose Trueheart
5/22

Print ISBN: 978-0-578-37618-9

I dedicate this book to my husband Jeffrey and our children, Courtney and Brandon. These wonderful people, my family, are the embodiment of Black Love for me. They have helped to fulfill my hopes, dreams, and my life overall, with joy. Together, by virtue of our existence, we have shown others that Black love and the Black family is real and something to strive for, with legacy as the ultimate outcome. For me, there has been no greater experience, than the Black Love that I have known with these individuals. May it continue with God's grace, as our lives move forward.

Contents

Contents

Acknowledgements

Expressing gratitude is a daily practice for me. I begin by thanking my husband, Jeffrey Rose Trueheart, for his loving commitment to me, always, and for seeing this project through with never-ending support. He is my first and only reader/editor before final publication review. I appreciate his attention to detail and for giving me his loving, intelligent, honest feedback.

I also thank my children, Courtney and Brandon. I am profoundly moved by them and the wonderful adults they have become. As a Professor and Lawyer, respectively, they both inspire me based on their realities in the midst of an increasingly complicated world. Their generation, bombarded by technology, and their myriad experiences navigating recent global challenges, helped me to see them, as deep thinkers who have the ability to discern information with clarity, questions and answers. Courtney, our first born, is a gifted Visiting Professor at the University where I started my academic career, when she was a little girl. She earned her doctorate at Teachers College, Columbia University, where I also earned mine, when she was two years old. I am filled with pride to watch her walk in my footsteps. Brandon is an accomplished Attorney, General Counsel-US Litigation, for a large firm. Watching him serve as a professional with such skill and adeptness also fills

Acknowledgements

me with pride, as he attended, undergraduate school, Yale University, like his father and I (graduate school where I earned my Master's Degree). These full circle moments that create our family history and legacy, are what gave me the insight and understanding to complete this work about Black love with joy and perseverance.

Gratitude is also expressed to Dr. Annie Daniel for the information that she provided for the chapter about Ghana, based on her experience there. I also want to thank all of the interviewees in this book, namely, my husband, Mr. Jeffrey Rose Trueheart, Dr. Anthony Munroe, Mr. DeQuan Jones, Mr. Hubert Peterson, Mr. and Mrs. Rahel and Maurice Arrington, Mrs. Maya Posey-Pierre and Mr. Marc Pierre. I am extremely appreciative that they took the time to speak with me about Black love, with such candor, dignity and grace. The time that they devoted to speak with me, in depth, added the necessary voices to this book.

Finally, and above all, I thank God. There is definitely a force in my life that is greater than my mind can imagine that leads, guides, and protects me and my treasured Black family. I am humbly grateful for the Black love in my life, as I believe that as Black people, we need it to sustain our endurance.

Acknowledgements

Within the context of this understanding, I always lean on the strength and courage of God, and doing so has never failed me.

Preface

Over the past two years, a slogan emerged, in the midst of a very tumultuous time. Simply stated, "We are all in this together" is the oft repeated phrase that we hear in the media and beyond. In my mind, the slogan expressed unity, which led me to think about Black people and how this was resonating with us. It translated for me, to Black Love. I began to think of all of the struggles that Black people have been through in this nation and throughout the world, from slavery to colonization, and the liberties that we have in this nation, filled with chaos and struggles, over many generations and laced with accomplishments and success. I have always wanted to write a book to explore how we have always been in this together, with fragile unity, that needs to be strengthened. The strength is a very powerful concept. It is Black love.

This book begins by asking the complex question, *What is Black love?* It is not an easy question to answer, but it is tackled in this work, with an attempt to explain it with grace and fortitude. The goal is not to isolate Black people from others, but rather to explain the importance

Preface

of Black people learning to love each other in marriage, as parents, as children towards parents, as adults who must respect elders and the building of legacy for future generations of Black people. This Introductory chapter is followed by one of six interviews. The first interview, entitled *Atlanta Newlyweds* is about a delightful couple, married only briefly, thus far. Their love exudes from the pages and it is not possible to read their words and not actually feel Black love. They make it a tangible experience for the reader.

The chapter that follows is an explanation about Black fathers. It demystifies the notion that Black fathers are missing by referring to this as a myth. Black fathers are not missing in the true sense of that word. We know where they are, but the question is why are they considered missing? The answer is because they are mass incarcerated, isolated from their families by government policies and beyond. But most importantly, when they are present, they are fully there with their children and families. We need to better understand what is happening with Black men, so that we can love them back into our hearts and minds, but most importantly, our lives. An interview follows this chapter, with a very dynamic, deep brother, who is parenting his sons with intense, abiding love, that will warm your heart, as he discusses his two little boys, who he refers to as his heartbeats. I asked him why he uses such a term to describe them and his answer epitomizes Black love. He is not a missing Black father, although he cannot always be with them for reasons beyond his control. My hope is that his interview will serve as a salient example of what Black love is for a Black man who is fathering two Black boys, in a society that does not necessarily see them as beautiful.

It is not possible to understand Black love, without taking a look at the roots of Black people. The soil of Black people begins in Africa, largely, West Africa. A nation was chosen that is emblematic, in an attempt to remind us of the connection between Black people in America and Black people in Africa, and some basic commonalities. This chapter is handled by Dr. Annie

Preface

Daniel, who in a very cursory, outline format, provides brief insight from her study abroad experience in Africa while a student. She highlights some key points, based on observational research, as a glimpse into some core similarities that help us to know that in truth, we are one and the same with our African brothers and sisters, merely living on different continents, due to circumstances beyond our control, namely slavery. Her information is not to be treated as an academic treatise but a mere glimpse, through her lens, while visiting Ghana. I, too, visited Ghana with my family, in 2019, during the Year of Return, which I discuss briefly in this book. This was one of my many trips to Africa, and I know that I am an African, living in America, hence an American too. I embrace that fact, wholeheartedly, in the context of Black love.

This glimpse into our African roots is followed by an interview with a man that I love and cherish. He is my husband of 36 plus years, at this point. I interviewed him as objectively as possible to try to find out what Black love means to him, within the context of our family, and

Preface

as a Black man in general. We sat at a table, in our kitchen nook area, and cozily chatted as I queried, recorded and listened to his responses. It was a beautiful moment, I must say, to hear my husband talk about Black love as it pertains to him, me and our precious children, who are adults. Nothing he said surprised me, because I know him and what he is about as a Black man. He destroys the myth of the missing Black father as it would not be possible to be more present than this man, in terms of his family. Oddly, he had to find his own father, a complicated story, which led to our recently changing our names to his, which is Trueheart. How telling that name is, which is why as a writer, you see my former last name, Rose, with the addition of my new last name, Trueheart. How befitting that new name is, at this time, when I decided to write about Black love. We are true hearts, in every sense of those words. It is not possible for me to consider what my life would have been like without my husband in it. We are Black love.

Following this chapter, a statement is made with the title, *Black Love is the Answer.* The answer to what, may be

Preface

the question, which is delicately explored with details to ensure that you understand. At the end of that chapter, I take the opportunity to write letters to various facets of Black people, namely the Black mother, the Black Father, the Black woman, who may or may not have children, and the Black man, who may or may not have children. These are proverbial letters, not specific to any one person, so read them from that perspective. Hopefully, they will inspire more letters, for the sake of communication about our deepest feelings, within the context of Black love.

I assure you, in the interview that follows, that you will absolutely enjoy what this young, husband and father has to say. His words are heartwarming and express Black love to the core. I do not want to go into it here, for fear of interfering with the candor with which he speaks about the love for his wife and daughter. He is a professional athlete, committed to his work and skill, but there is no comparison to the depth of his understanding and lived experience in Black love. His interview is absolutely delicious!

Preface

The next chapter, followed by two more interviews, is about Sankofa, an Adrinka term referring to returning and getting it. We must return and get Black love, unabashedly, unashamedly, without judgement and explanations. It is a beautiful thing, heterosexually speaking, which is my vantage point, for a Black man and Black woman to marry, have Black children and build a life together, making Black history and creating legacies to carry on for generations. The first interview that follows this chapter is entitled *NYC Newlyweds*. This couple is absolutely adorable, brilliant, and they exude intelligence as they explain their Black love and how and why they chose each other. I felt something deep when I interviewed them. Through their voices, laughter and serious tones, I had the experience, beyond my own personal relationship with my husband, of knowing the beauty of Black love. Their interview is a moment in time to cherish, filled with hope and best wishes for the two of them, as they are just getting started. There is a sense that Black love will endure for them, as is the case for the story told in the last interview.

Preface

There is something to be said about saving the best for last. In this case, the best is defined as longevity. The Black man interviewed in the last chapter had been married to his wife for 39 years, at the time of the interview. That number has risen to 40 years since then. He has two beautiful daughters, now adults, who he talks about with deep fondness as a consummate father, detailing the ways that he cared for them throughout their lives. He speaks of his enduring love for his wife and family and how Black love happened for them, including break-ups before their marriage and sustaining their marriage for many, many years, afterwards. I felt it befitting to close the interviews with this one because it epitomizes Black love. It teaches us, it is illustrative and most importantly, it explains to us that the Black father is not missing. As time progresses, we can ignore that oft mentioned commentary about Black men and instead search and find in our hearts and minds, Black love as present and the sustenance needed for our survival, in a world that does not see us as who we truly are but what others think we are. We are Black love and always will be.

Preface

Finally, I close this book with a list of ingredients and affirmations, to enhance the recipe of Black love. These are not requirements but merely considerations when you are thinking about what you might do to make your Black love experience better. My mother was a fantastic, southern cook. I write about her within these pages. I used to watch her work her in the kitchen. She rarely used a recipe and would often express how you merely need to add a pinch of this or a handful of that and the result of whatever dish she was making was magic. I captured her ingredients, before she passed away, and so now I have her "recipes," captured in my book entitled "*Effie's Soul Food Recipes with a Healthy Twist.*" I know that the essence of what she did in the kitchen could never be captured on paper, because every meal she cooked was made with Black love. Thus, the ingredients that close this book, along with brief affirmations that follow, are merely a pinch of this and a handful of that, but the essence, is Black Love.

One

♥

What Is Black Love?

Black Love Is the Answer for Black People

Recently, a young Black, former student of mine, DeQuan Jones, after I interviewed him for this book, said "Black Love Is the Answer for Black people." His statement resonated with me and is a wonderful way to continue this conversation. Black love is a unique understanding, between two Black people, of the experience of being Black in this nation, the United States of America. This understanding is probably true in many places in the world, but given that my long-term living experiences have been in this nation, it is what I know. Black love is about being comfortable in all kinds of spaces, as indicated by another interviewee in this book. It is the way that many of us were raised, in the midst of constantly being reminded of our race, in so many ways, in this nation. Our skin and hair texture immediately

1

identifies us as Black. Although seemingly far removed, it makes us keenly aware that our ancestors (particularly for Black Americans) were probably slaves in this nation, and that we are their descendants. For Caribbean, Brazilian and other Black people living in the United States, now, their ancestors were probably slaves in the countries of their family lineage or perhaps where they were born, if not in the United States. Many people want us to forget slavery and many Black people have completely disconnected from that reality, but truly it is undeniable. That truth literally runs through our veins.

Connecting with another Black person, in love, and bringing new Black babies into this world, and teaching them all that you know and have experienced, as Black adults, including the good, the bad and the ugly, will help them navigate through a society where they may feel displaced at some point in their lives. Perhaps not right away, but somewhere within their lives, they may look around and suddenly realize that they are being treated differently, that they are having a different experience than their white counterparts in the same spaces, that the

WHAT IS BLACK LOVE?

food they are eating is different, along with the type of music they are listening to and so much more. This book, however, is not a jaunt into a discussion of critical race theory or Diversity, Equity, and Inclusion (DEI), or to send us on a sojourn of division, and distraction by those who disagree, on any basis, based on anyone's analysis, but rather a treatise about love, namely Black Love, and the humanity associated with this type of union in a very diverse world.

I remember, as a young Black girl in elementary school, attending a predominantly white school where most of my classmates were so nice to me. But they would often ask me questions about my hair because it was very different from theirs. I do not think I had paid that much attention to it because my mother kept my hair pressed and curled rather than allowing it to be kinky. I preferred the kinky curls but my mother abhorred it. I later learned that this was a form of assimilation that she imposed on me as I would have had an afro, if my hair was allowed to be free. One of those white classmates was my best friend. One year, my mother actually made our dresses for our class picture and we wore those yellow dresses proudly, as my mother was an excellent seamstress. Although my mother was not fond of allowing me to participate in sleepovers, she allowed me to do so at my friend's home one evening. I noticed something right away. That girl and her siblings were able to speak to their mother in a very unruly way. It was shocking when I witnessed her telling her mother to shut-up to her face. I literally thought to myself that if I ever spoke to my mother that way, I would not survive it as my mother would, as she would put it, "tear that ass up." Now that sounds awful, I know, but it was understood, among every Black friend that I knew, that you never, ever disrespect your parents or there would be serious consequences.   This was not understood as a negative, but as a form of Black love—teaching you respect, discipline and how to honor your parents. That carried on into adulthood and until my mother was placed in her grave. I knew what tone to use and how to speak to her.

Although mere examples of Black love, there is a recognition of some commonalities that Black people generally have. This is not an attempt to stereotype, but rather to identify generalities as clearly households vary. However, there are some codes or concepts that we intrinsically understand about each other and when we stray away from that, we know we are doing so. Deep down inside, we know that although we are Americans, we are also Africans and when we can connect on that level, without societal interference, it feels very real. There is an understanding between each other, particularly in marriage and in our intimate relationships, whether they ultimately are long term or not, that there is an intrinsic connection and a level of comfort that in the right circumstances, works out perfectly, leading to recollections of Black history together and the creation of Black family legacies.

Black Love Is Survival

In this society, on so many levels, Black people have to learn how to survive, from cradle to grave, as all people do. However, for Black people, it becomes difficult for many because resources may be more limited than is the case for other groups. Therefore, a mentality must arise, that includes basic instincts, about how to make it. Making it refers to getting through K-12 school, perhaps going to college or choosing some other alternative that will lead to sufficient income, going to graduate school, paying for such higher education, finding a partner to love when, especially for Black women, this is a challenge (for myriad reasons discussed elsewhere in this book), getting and keeping a job and rising to similar heights, career-wise. This is not due to capabilities, but other factors to be discussed. If any of that transpires successfully and children are born to Black couples, ensuring that they can navigate the same process, with the least amount of difficulty becomes the next challenge. There may also be the scenario of some Black couples having to take care of parents, who may have struggled all of their lives, with limited resources. The survival aspect is so deep that I would be doing a disservice if I tried to cover it completely here. Some may read what I am saying here and think that I am not expressing anything that is different for any other group of people or individual humans in general. Perhaps that is right, but there is no doubt that there are some unique experiences inherent in the fact that one's existence emerged out of enslavement on this soil and that although it was 400 plus years ago, it happened. There are times when one thinks about it, learns about it and has to process it, even though society says to negate these thoughts because it happened in the past and has no bearing on your current life. Some Black people believe that. However, we are not in a post-racial society, no matter how much we want that, and coming to terms with that reality can be a very poignant awakening, if we allow it to be.

The reality is that if Black people join together in love relationships, marriage, having their babies together, and walk this society in unity, we will have a better chance of survival and so will our children, grandchildren and generations to come. This includes emphasizing education, increasing earning potential, taking care of each other in sickness and health, sharing knowledge and information with each other, trusting and protecting each other, in all walks of life, along with additional Black people that are brought into these unions such as daughter-in-laws, son-in laws and their families. As we build together, in unity, we will have a better chance of survival together. In this process, we create legacy, passing on all that we garner, from our love, history and our finances, to the next generation and then further. Through this process, survival will be less challenging and our legacies will be more fortuitous in every way.

What Can Black People in this Nation Show the World?

When I was growing up, there were, ultimately, television shows that depicted Black people including The Jeffersons, Sanford and Son, Good Times and a few others. These were sitcoms, with a great deal of humor, drama, and stereotypes, that showed me and other children like me, Black family units in the United States, outside of my own family. It was nice to see because, before those shows came about, I would turn on the television and there were shows that only depicted white people. Black people were often shown only as servants

WHAT IS BLACK LOVE?

as white people were living in beautiful homes, traveling and doing all kinds of exciting things. I remember a show that I used to watch about a white girl named Gidget. Gidget had all white friends. They traveled to Europe and other places, enjoyed the beach, surfed, and experienced life with a sense of relaxed joy, with very few problems. My childhood was very nice but Gidget's experience was so carefree, while she was being unapologetically white. This made a tremendous impression on me, because it was that sense of also being carefree, while being unapologetically Black, that I wanted. This may be one of the many reasons that I have traveled to over 50 countries, with my husband, and to many of those places with our children, and made decisions about my higher education and career that were based on my idea of what I felt gave me the most freedom and joy.

As Black people, I guess one salient feature that we can show the world is that besides our intelligence, our excellent capabilities in scholarship, research, inventions and outstanding contributions in nearly every field, including science, medicine, the law, athletics and the Arts, we also enjoy being carefree and love each other as much as any other group loves its people. Black people protest, struggle, speak about our experiences, as Black people trying to survive in this society and beyond, but we also enjoy being relaxed and enjoying the finer things in life, unashamedly. We can do that while loving our people, of which many are continually oppressed and need help, while we also enjoy living in highly resourced neighborhoods. I know that to some, that may seem materialistic, but we live in a capitalist society. Money is a big part of that way of life. Prosperity and abundance is a goal that should not lead to one feeling guilty or ashamed if it is desired/attained. The world is full of and based on abundance and every human being should have full and free access to it, unashamedly.

Often times, when I am enjoying an opulent place while traveling or even locally, as I sip a glass of wine, with a book or magazine that I am enjoying reading while basking in the afternoon sun, after a long swim, I realize that this is a mere example of carefree behavior, that we must show the world, in addition to our fight for equity for all Black and oppressed people. Let us show the world the non-suffering humanity of Black people, as we strive for equity, which many believe we already have and should not discuss. I will never understand why the word equity makes some people upset. We deserve to be prosperous, abundant and carefree too, as many of us are. Enjoying our lives together, in a state of joy, is a key aspect of Black love.

Exercise I

Creating a Family Tree and Black Love Energy Radiation

Find a comfortable space to sit, write and think. Choose two pieces of paper and pens as there is something about brain to hand writing, with a pen and paper, that makes the process intuitive. Use colored pens if you have them, with as much color variation as possible. You should take as much time as you need to complete this exercise.

--On your first sheet of paper, draw a tree—a simple tree, with as many branches as necessary as you proceed.

-- Go back as far as you can, identifying members of your family, branching out with lines until you get to your father and mother. Have fun with this. You do not have to be an artist. Just create lines as branches, as you see them.

--Put questions marks where you do not have names of family members for your branches and write down, on a separate piece of paper, living family members that you can contact, in the future, to help you fill in the blanks.

Exercise II

Creating Your Inner Circle

--Once your tree is complete, to your comfort level, move forward to the next step which is the creation of concentric circles on another piece of paper.

--Start with an inner circle (the nucleus of your Black family). In the inner circle (the nucleus), include your mother, your father and your siblings (if you have any) even if these people were not present or currently in your life.

--Draw a circle around the inner circle (nucleus) and include the names of your closest relatives outside of your nuclear family (your extended family). This group should include cousins, aunts, uncles and beyond but they must be family. Write their names or nicknames, essentially, whatever names you prefer to refer to them. Include those relatives who may not be currently in your life, if you choose that you want them in your circle.

--Draw the outer circle, around the extended family circle, and include people that are not related to you. This should include Black friends, colleagues/acquaintances. Choose only those people that you truly want in your circle. They must not be relatives from the other two circles.

--From each name in your circles draw an arrow from their names, radiating out beyond the outer circle, into the universal space. Those arrows represent energy radiating out from the nucleus (your center) beyond your circles; the energy of Black love, radiating out, from you, to the rest of the world.

Black Love Is Energy

One thing that we must realize, as Black people, is that we are energy and thus, all connected to each other and the world. We are connected by virtue of our lineage as children of Africa and as energetic beings. The first connection that we experience as humans is to our nuclear families, no matter how complete or incomplete. Then, we connect to our extended family, non-familial significant people in our lives and then people at large (all people). Our nucleus is our power and where there is true Black love it is absolutely unconditional. We can always use that power by absorbing it, cherishing it, connecting to it and letting it go in and out of us, in the form of energy even when some in the nucleus are no longer physically with us. We can still draw on their ancestral power, when they depart from the physical plane. These people are the essence of our Black Love, which is the positive energy flow, from our core. Look at your family

WHAT IS BLACK LOVE?

tree and concentric circles often, as a reminder of the many branches with a common root and your nucleus (center) surrounded by those in your circles. As you look at your family tree remember to never forget your roots. As you look at the nucleus, remember, therein lies unconditional love and your power. With these types of foundations, no matter where you go and what you experience in life, you will feel grounded in Black Love.

Two

Atlanta Newlyweds

Newlywed Black couples often find themselves in a learning process with each other, as they navigate through society, together, in a whirlwind of events that impact the Black community, oftentimes within the context of harsh realities, news-wise. This musical couple candidly share their story with energy and fervor, without shying away from the fact that they are figuring it out as they are going along. It was a delight to hear them talk about their Black love because it is fresh and, as a result, you can feel the tenderness of their love for each other, their enjoyment of the present, and their hopes for the future. I hope you enjoy their story as much as I enjoyed interviewing them as their words give us all an opportunity to understand Black Love as a new beginning for two people who found each other, by chance, and plan to spend their lives together.

ATLANTA NEWLYWEDS

Rahel (Rah) and Maurice (Reece) Arrington

Reece and Rah are two Atlanta based music creatives, who recently got married and decided to share their journey in finding love in a modern world. Rah is a graduate of the University of Miami, where she studied psychology, and is currently a Disc Jockey (DJ). She is originally from Oakland, California. Maurice is a graduate of Frostburg University, where he studied business, and is currently a Music Producer. He is originally from Hagerstown, MD.

Rah and Reece

A RETURN TO BLACK LOVE

Rose Trueheart: How long have you been married? Where did you meet? Either of you can answer these questions.

Reese: We have been married for four months. We met on May 18, 2017.

Rose Trueheart: Okay, so you are literally newlyweds. That is beautiful. That is so wonderful. I think of all the interviewees for this book, you have been married for the shortest amount of time. So, this is perfect. Now, where did you meet?

Rah: We met in Atlanta, Georgia. I am a DJ and Maurice is a producer, and we both happened to be performing at the same event on May 18 and we both got there and it was love at first sight.

Reece: Yeah. We both got there early. We set up across from each other, I guess just going over whatever personal things we were going to perform and I saw her directly across from me and I made my presence known. I went over and introduced myself.

Rose Trueheart: Rahel, you were my excellent Student Assistant. I saw, after graduation, ultimately, you became a DJ. I just think that is the coolest, most wonderful thing, because I thought you were thinking of becoming an Event Coordinator, if I am not mistaken. I absolutely remember you because you were so helpful to me juggling all of those students at the University of Miami. It is very fascinating to me that you went from your particular goal, while a student, to becoming a DJ. Can you just tell me just a tiny bit about that, so we can understand how you made that transition because that is so interesting?

Rah: Yeah, so I have always had an affinity for music. When I graduated from the University of Miami, it was right in the middle of the recession, where there really was not a lot of job opportunities. I found myself back in school for my Masters. In an attempt to jump to something outside of the box, I said, you know what, why not? I was working in higher education at the time, and I decided to go to Guitar Center and purchase turntables to see how far it would take me. It started off as an experiment and then it got me so many opportunities. I was able to fly to Japan, I have been on tour, and I have

19

been able to meet really cool celebrities and artists and I have been having the time of my life.

Rose Trueheart: That is so fantastic! Reece you are a Music Producer? Is that correct?

Reece: Correct. I am a Music Producer. I think I am starting to get into some other areas of producing as well, but for now, I will stay with the title, Music Producer.

Rose Trueheart: That is a match made in heaven; a perfect match. A Music Producer and a DJ. Let's move on to question number two. Did you consciously choose to marry a Black person? And if so, why? If not, why?

Rah: Yes, I consciously chose to marry a Black person. I am not opposed to dating outside of the race. I have dated outside of my race. However, as I got older, I realized how I wanted to live my life and what was going on around me in my community. I just thought about my family and my legacy and how if I wanted to help change the narrative of our people and that I wanted to start by marrying someone that looked like me to make that happen.

Rose Trueheart: Okay. Reece, how about you?

Reece: As for me, I definitely chose to marry Black. Again, like Rahel, I do not have any opposition or problem with interracial dating at all. But, when I think about certain things like my big sister and my mother and like, just the things that Black women do for us as Black men automatically, I do not know that any other race of women would do that. It is things like, you find yourself in trouble. Your big sister is going to let you stay on the couch. She is going to do whatever it takes to make sure you get back on your feet. I just do not know that any other race of women has the same empathy for us and it just makes more sense to me.

Rose Trueheart: Okay. Let's move on to the next question, . You have been married for a short time. What do you think will contribute to a lasting union? Just give me a couple of factors.

Rah: Well, we both really, really, really over communicate even when it is uncomfortable. We did premarital counseling, and it is the art of oversharing. It is even when you do not feel like talking, about it. Of course, it is all new. But our Therapist advised us to communicate, to be extremely honest, brutally honest.

Reece: I think forgiveness, even when somebody does not ask for forgiveness, is extremely important. I think apologizing, even when you feel like you are right and you do not feel like apologizing. It is extremely important. I think that effort is the last and final piece because like every now and then Rah will definitely try to show me up on date night and do something that is so amazing and I am just like, what am I going to do next? It is just effort. It is not perfection. I can tell you that Rah is a better planner than me but I am trying to catch up. I am trying to level up. It does not feel like a bad competition but there is a competition in effort for each other sometimes. I think that is important.

Rose Trueheart: Yes. Okay. As someone who's been married for 36 years, so far, so good.

Rah: We are on the right track.

Rose Trueheart: Just the fact that you said date night is very important because my husband and I, still to this day, have a date night every Friday. It is a beautiful thing.

Let's go on to number four. What does quality time with each other mean to you?

Rah: Quality time means putting away distractions. Today is our quality time day, doing this interview, or even our podcast. Just putting away distractions and focusing on each other. Whether it is date night or planning a trip. Recently, we went on a trip for my birthday and that was 100% quality time. We have very, very, very, very busy lives, and we can go days sometimes just run, run and run. But we make it a point to stop and say, Hey, I see you. Are you good? Let's spend a little bit of time together.

Rose Trueheart: Excellent.

Reece: Yeah, I feel like she kind of just said everything that I kind of feel. Distraction free is I think the most important thing. At the end of the day, I think I am really grateful to have a partner that enjoys a lot of the same things that I enjoy. So, obviously, not right now, but if it were not a pandemic, we'd be going to shows. We go out to eat a lot. We are foodies. We are spirit and cocktail nerds and just lying on the couch together, is great to me.

A RETURN TO BLACK LOVE

Rose Trueheart: Excellent. Okay, we are going on to number five. As a Black couple, do you think that there are any unique aspects to your marriage relative to other groups? And on top of that, who is most actively involved in activities that are domestic in the household, like cooking and cleaning the house? I need examples.

Rah: I think that what makes us stand out is the fact that it is not as common in our culture as it should be. What we realized when we got married and even when we started dating and we were public, because a lot of our generation, I would say we are elderly millennials, does not really showcase Black love as much as our parents do. When we went public with our love, our marriage, our dating and everything, the number one thing we got from our supporters and people who know us was wow, what you guys have is real and we wish we saw more of it. But we quickly realized that it was not common to find what we had. What we had was rare. I guess that answers the first part of your question.

Rose Trueheart: Yes. Reece, your thoughts?

ATLANTA NEWLYWEDS

Reece: What I feel is unique about us as a Black couple is because of the way that we were raised and because of all of the many, many circumstances that Black people go through, I feel like we are good anywhere. I think that is not necessarily something that everybody might feel. We are comfortable in pretty much any situation. We are comfortable being in corporate spaces. We are comfortable in white spaces. We are comfortable in hood areas. We are comfortable in hood areas out of the country. We find our way. We find ways to make friends with everybody, everywhere that we go. I do not think that everybody necessarily can feel all that comfortable in that. I feel the reason why we are comfortable in that, is because we are a Black couple with so many different experiences. I think that is exactly why we are comfortable everywhere.

Rose Trueheart: Okay, great. Let's get to the next part of that question. Who is most actively involved in domestic activities around the house such as cooking and cleaning, and all of those things. I need a couple of examples.

25

A RETURN TO BLACK LOVE

Rah: So, I am going to say 60% Maurice is domestic, 40% me, which is a surprise, but I hate cooking and I hate cleaning. I do it and I am the better cook in the family but Reece loves to,

every morning, the first 15 minutes of his day before his day gets started, to make sure that the kitchen is clean, which is awesome. Yeah, I am not that person.

Rose Trueheart: I love that, honestly. Reece, do you want to add to that at all?

Reece: You know it is interesting because I do not think that when I was a bachelor, I was all that cleanly. I think that all of a sudden, my mother kicked in. Now, I just find myself on autopilot. I do not mind it every day. It is kind of meditative to me.

Rose Trueheart: All right. As a Black couple, do you think that history, lineage and legacy are important in terms of your relationship and your future together? If so, how?

Reece: I love that question. I will go first. My family is such a huge family. Right. I want to say that, my mother's father, my grandfather, on that side, there was something like 14-15 kids. It could even be more than that. My family is huge. Our family tree is huge. We trace back the whole way to great, great grandma. We have got pictures and stories, and photo books and photo albums and everything. I am really glad that Rah is the person that documents everything. I am not that great with documenting things. But, when I look back on my family, I look back on all those pictures, I think it is extremely important to be able to tell the stories about where we came from. My mother is somebody who can talk for hours about things that I would never know. It is not a problem. It is a joy to sit around and listen to her talk about it.

Rah: For me, I will be very honest and transparent. I never wanted a family until I met Maurice. Although I have a great family and I love my sisters and my mom and my dad, because of a lot of my past trauma associated with certain things that I have gone through, I really never saw myself being a mother and carrying on the lineage for myself. Then when I started dating Maurice, we started talking about our future, and I saw the type of man that he is and how he treats me as a woman and how he treats the people around him. He is just an overall amazing human. I immediately was like, wow, I would love to continue that. I would love to create more humans like the man that I met and that was when I started thinking about lineage. We are four months in having those conversations, preparing to have children and what's that going to look like? I am very excited about that.

Rose Trueheart: Well, that is wonderful. I was not going to ask you that question, about children, because you have been married for such a short time but I am glad you brought that up because part of that question is legacy. In terms of Black people, we have to think about, not just the present, but also the future and what kind of legacy are we looking toward. I believe that you both answered that. I appreciate it because legacy is important for our people too. You know what I am saying? Okay, so let's move on. What message would you offer to young Black couples, who are dating and thinking of marriage at some point in the near or distant future?

ATLANTA NEWLYWEDS

Reece: The advice that I offer to anybody who thinks they want to get serious about anything in life, but especially a relationship, is to be 1,000% honest with yourself. You cannot come into this situation, trying to finesse your partner by hiding certain aspects of yourself. It is never going to work. You have to be able to be 100% authentically yourself. I think sometimes people need to go find what that is before they decide to commit to another person. If you can be your authentic self, and that does not mean that you do not strive to be better, or you do not change certain things or reach a little bit higher. If you cannot be authentically 100% yourself with your partner, I do not think you are going to be happy. I think that at some point, things will start to unravel.

Rah: To that point, I will add, just be prepared to unpack the difficult conversations that we never want to have. Those conversations are our roadmap to healing. A lot of times, we do not realize some of the things that we are hiding until we are in front of another person and that other person holds up a mirror to us so you can see who you really are and we shy away from it. Sometimes we self-sabotage and we kind of ruin relationships because of that. But if you are wanting a healthy, successful relationship, you have to be prepared to have those conversations not only with yourself, but with your partner.

Rose Trueheart: Excellent. So smart. I am just very impressed. I already knew this going in because I remember you, Rahel, as my student too. I can hear that you are the same, but yet you have matured and you are so intellectually capable. I think that you have found a person in your life that offers the same characteristics. This is just wonderful to hear. Let's go on. What are the most important aspects of marriage from your vantage point? This is different from the question I asked previously.

Reece: Okay, so I have got it. I have got a few. I feel like this could kind of be like an umbrella answer. I will give one answer. I think the most important aspect of marriage for me is accountability that you have, being with another person. There is also this feeling that I am not alone, which is extremely important. As one example

ATLANTA NEWLYWEDS

I went to the emergency room, a few weeks ago. Just having her, she could not come in, of course, because it is Covid right now, but just knowing that somebody was waiting for me, knowing that somebody was worried for me, when somebody was texting my phone constantly checking on me, was this whole different thing. You got family, you got people now. I have got my people but like as a single grown man, I was not calling my mother for certain situations, right? But now I have got somebody in my corner all the time.

Rose Trueheart: Excellent. Okay, so your most important aspect is accountability. That is a very interesting and compelling answer. Okay, what about you Rahel? I hear that you refer to each other as Reese and Rah. I do not know if I should be calling you Rahel at this point. But I am just so used to saying that name for you.

Rah: Oh no. That is so funny. Honestly, when people call me Rahel, I know that you have known me for a long time. Rah is the persona, that has developed over the last couple of years.

Rose Trueheart: Yeah, so that means we go way back. I got it. Okay, well, go ahead.

Rah: My answer to that question is transparency because I feel like transparency comes with honesty, trust and communication. I feel like when you are transparent with your partner, you are not allowing room for error. You trust that person to hold your heart. In sharing with that person and communicating with a person your highs and lows. If you are transparent with that person, truly, truly transparent, it is as if you are standing naked in the mirror, looking at yourself. That could be very good for your relationship.

Rose Trueheart: Okay, excellent. So, accountability and transparency. I see how you squeezed in three things Rahel. Did you see that Reece? She was slick, right? She took her response and put it into three parts. That was slick. Let's go on. Do you think that educational level matters relative to each other? Should couples who plan to marry or who are married consider this?

Rah: I will go first. Yes, I definitely think education level matters. We both have bachelor's degrees. But I will also say that education does not have to necessarily be traditional. One thing about Maurice that I fell in love with was that even though on paper, I have more degrees than him, I felt like he was smarter than me, because he is a book reader. The man has read so many books, I cannot even keep up with them about topics that you normally would not find a Black man reading about. I have to say that if you meet a person who is constantly seeking knowledge in any type of way, and that meets you and what you are trying to grow to, then absolutely go for it. It does not necessarily have to mean they have to have two degrees and have to make a certain salary. No. As long as they are furthering their education in some capacity, whether it is traditional or non-traditional and that is what you feel works best for you then I say that could lead to a successful relationship.

Reece: I agree, I think educational level is extremely important. But I think the different type of education is not always about the things that you can put on paper, right? I think that as long as you have a like mind and as long as you have a spirit that is open to being shaken up and being wrong and could be improved, you know, to just receive more, then I think that is a great space to be in because you can do right from that space. There is no telling where you get in. I do not want to downplay how important actual education is. I think that is important as well.

Rose Trueheart: I am glad you said that. Let's go in there just a little bit, because I want to make sure it is understood because this is a question that is asked of everyone in these interviews. Let me add another word or two to the question. Do you think that higher education level matters? For example, if a person finishes at a high school diploma level and another person has a Bachelor's degree, does that work?

Reece: I think it is kind of hard for two people to match up. If you do not seek that and you are content, and not trying to reach out a little bit higher, I think it would be harder. I think it is hard on people in two different spaces. I do not think you should be, if not evenly matched up, you should be somewhat matched up, and that there should be some hunger, some questions and some openness for a little bit more.

Rose Trueheart: Okay. Rahel, do you agree?

Rah: Yes. I agree.

Rose Trueheart: Ok. So that is agreement. That was a very thorough answer. Thank you. This is our last question. It is a two-part question. Do you have any parting thoughts about Black love and do you have any pearls of wisdom that you want to share? I know you have only been married for four months, but you have some wisdom there. So, let's hear it. Okay?

Reece: So, to me, as a Black man, I think that Black Love is the thing that is going to sustain you in the world. It is so many different things and so many different fears. There are so many different things that happen to you, in the course of just every day, living your life. I think that having Black love in your corner is that one place that you feel understood. I think that for me, that is why it is extremely important. The best piece of wisdom that I think that I have to offer, and I do not even know that I am wise yet, is to not just be in something or doing something for yourself. If you can react to anger slowly, then please react to anger slowly. If you can apologize first, go apologize first and be the bigger person. None of that is anything that is self-serving. Like it is not. I think a lot of times people want to think about what's in it for me, or how's this person treating me? Or is this person good for me? I think you really need to think are you good for anybody else, probably first.

Rose Trueheart: That sounds like wisdom.

Rah: Yeah. I do not know how I am going to go after that. When it comes to Black love, and for anybody that is seeking it, and why it is so important, it really, truly begins with self. I feel like as a Black community, Black people, we have a lot of healing to do. And the reason why it is not as easy as we wish is because we have a hard time recognizing the healing that we need to do within ourselves. I would always start there, when it comes to, how do I get what you have? I guess that is what we get a lot. It starts with yourself. Do you love yourself, because if you want to love on somebody else, the only way to be able to do that is if you love on yourself, and then that

that is how it goes? Love is contagious. That love that is shared between two people starts with one and then turns into three and it turns into a whole tribe and then your legacy is created. So, in order for us to keep growing we have got to start with the first person and that is you.

Rose Trueheart: Great. That was your statement about love. Do you have any pearls of wisdom to add to that?

Rah: Yeah, well, like I combined.

Rose Trueheart: Yeah. Before she tried to spread it out and this time she tried to tighten it up, but you know who you are talking to Rahel. So, let me hear those pearls of wisdom.

Rah: Pearls of wisdom? Wow. I am new to this so I feel that wisdom is yet to come. But I always consider what I have done and I tell people to go to people who have had been there, done that. So, for example, you and your husband have been married for 36 years. My mom, before my father passed, was married for 18 years. I go to her to be fortified. Do not ever hesitate to lean on those who've been there and done that for the teaching because those nuggets are what you can apply and take to make your relationship better.

Rose Trueheart: Okay, so I knew it was there. That is why I pulled for it. That was absolutely beautiful. As for the overall interview, that was fantastic. I really appreciate you both for doing this. Like I said, I am interviewing an array of individuals and so you are representing, along with one other couple, individuals who are newly married and who have not had children as of yet. This gives a unique perspective because some of the couples that I interviewed have young children and adult children. It is amazing to look at us as Black people across a full spectrum. You know what I am saying? Most of my books/work has been around health disparities, and maternal and child health and all of those kinds of issues. But this too, is as significant for us because if we do not start standing up and telling our stories about who we are, and what Black love means to us, society will tell the stories for us. My husband and I have traveled to over 50 countries in this world, including in North, South, East and West Africa. We, like the two of you, are people of

African descent. Our people have had a long history of Black love, but it has been distorted. So, you are helping me to tell the story of our people about Black love. I want to thank both of you. I know it is a tough time, and it is hectic but I really appreciate it, from my heart, that you took the time to speak with me.

Reece: A couple of things, really quick. You and your husband and the 50 places around the world, that is goals. Also, I really think that this interview, even though it was for you, this was not a bad way to spend part of my day.

Rose Trueheart: Oh, I am so glad to hear that. Thank you both so much!

Three

♥

The Myth of the Missing Black Father

When I decided to undertake this writing, primarily about Black love and Black parenting, I found myself in a very unexpected space. After being married for 36 years, I had a vision in my mind of beginning to grow older, after raising two wonderful children, a boy and a girl, who are quite successful, one a Lawyer and one a Professor. I feel quite accomplished as a mother and wife and basically I am waiting for the marriages of our adult children and our little Black grandchildren to be born, someday. There were so many twists and turns in raising our children, all quite wonderful, as we did so with a commitment that is beyond understanding. There has been nothing as precious to us, as parents, than our children. We love and adore them. Every aspect of our lives was completely about our children. If we traveled, we took them with us, throughout the globe, as little ones, all the way through young adulthood, as we wanted to expand their worldview. We were deeply involved in ensuring that they received the best possible education that we could muster for them by moving to heavily resourced neighborhoods, looking for diversity in the process, which was generally achieved, until our son went to private school, in high school. We knew from the time that they were born, that they were our heritage, our lineage, our legacy and that their lives would be the same for their children as we were for our parents, so we wanted to parent correctly and with fervor.

First and foremost, we wanted them to be happy, to thrive, and for them to have joyous childhood memories to cherish. As their mother, I feel that having them in my life has shown me a part of myself that touches and feels love in its purest form, because my love for them is pure, unconditional and a powerful force that gives me strength, when I am at my weakest. I think I realized this when I gave birth to them, naturally, but I did not understand, at that time, that I would carry that power of Black love for the rest of my life.

A RETURN TO BLACK LOVE

The family experience, early on, was just so beautiful, even though there were ups and downs that we could never have foreseen including the death of my parents and my husband's parents (his adopted father, which will be explained later). Their deaths were unexpected and deeply painful. This meant that our children only had their grandparents in their lives for a short period of time, since they left us when the children were fairly young. After surviving the trauma of losing these cherished people, especially the grandmothers, as a Black woman, I felt directionless and uncertain about fully understanding motherhood and all it entailed, but within me, the charge, drive and energy was there. I took pride in the fact, and still do, that I am a Black mother, with a Black husband and that we were raising our children in a society that does not always value the racial aspect of our humanity, in general.

Although my children are now full-fledged adults, and our family experience remains wondrous, we are having greater problems now in our society, racially, than what I knew as a child. I do not recall Black men and women being killed, with such frequency. There are so many that I cannot begin to list all of their names for fear that I would miss one of them, which would be tragic, because they all matter. Do not get me wrong. Racism and acts of violence were definitely happening in early points in my life, but I felt less in tune to it all because there was no social media, the news was not on 24/7 and when I heard about such happenings, it all seemed somewhat distant from my day-to-day reality, especially as a child.

In any event, often times, for reasons unknown to others, Black fathers may not be present all of the time, or at all, in the households where their children are raised, but they are around. Black fathers have had to figure out, whether they are able to be with or not be with their children consistently or at all, how to care for them. In many instances, they have had to learn how to live in this society in a way that is not ordinary in the eyes of many, because there are unimaginable strains and unfavorable scenarios in their lives, even when there is high socioeconomic status. Then, of course, there is the Black father that is ever-present, committed in every way, for the long-haul, no matter what, caring for his children, along-side his wife/mother of his children, for the duration of their lives. The latter is the story that our society does not discuss that much. Somehow, the story of the proverbial missing Black father is more exciting to talk about as compared to the Black father who is always there—physically present in his children's lives. It does not seem to fit the narrative often used to describe Black families in American society, as what we are most familiar with are stories of negativity about Black men and their lack of commitment to their families. It is within this context that I want to try to straighten some things out and truly talk about what is transpiring in this society with Black men and why we must, as Black women, love them back to us, no matter what our experiences were with our fathers, and Black men in general, rather than give up on them as they are indeed a worthy cause to ensure that the illustrious legacy, history and lineage of Black people continues. Black women must encourage Black men to be all that they can be and to strive, like any other race of people, to secure education or to identify and hone their unique skills, to ensure that they too experience prosperity and can be prepared to care for their Black families.

Essentially, the notion of the missing Black father is a myth. Per a study by the Centers for Disease Control and Prevention, as reported by the Los Angeles Times, Reyes (2013), "by most measures, Black fathers who live with their children are just as involved as other dads who live with their kids — or more so." The study found that of Black fathers living at home with their children, 79% assisted with bathing and dressing the kids, daily.[1] In comparison to white fathers, there is no statistically

---

[1] Reyes, Emily, Alpert. "Survey Finds Dads Defy Stereotypes About Black Fatherhood," *Los Angeles Times*. December 20, 2013, https://www.latimes.com/local/la-xpm-2013-dec-20-la-me-Black-dads-20131221-story.html

significant difference. The reality is that even if Black fathers are not living with their children they are as active as other fathers who do not live with their children. Unfortunately, there are more Black fathers living away from their children and the reasons why are what has to be understood.

We must begin by recognizing that institutionalized oppression contributes to the problems associated with the Black family. Some of the factors currently are depressed wages, discriminatory hiring practices, inequality in educational opportunities, chronic unemployment and mass incarceration. The latter has led to reimagination of the family structure. The outcome of mass incarceration is aunts, uncles, grandmothers, grandfathers and etc. stepping in to raise children when the parent(s) are locked away.

Furthermore, although there is an effort to negate the validity of slavery in terms of current day problems impacting Black families, the long-term implications cannot be overlooked. Per an interesting piece in the Washington Post, the following are some of the realities of slavery that contributed to the destruction of Black families: [2]

> Black nuclear families were torn apart.
>
> Black women were raped and traumatized.
>
> Black children, mothers and fathers were sold away from each other.
>
> Black men were brutalized for many reasons, including any interactions (alleged or otherwise) with white women.

None of the items listed above are excuses for Black men who were/are not present in the traditional nuclear family structure, but rather the reality of the situation,

---

[2] Smith, Denzel, Mychal. "The Dangerous Myth of The Missing Black Father," *Washington Post.* January 19, 2017, https://www.washingtonpost.com/posteverything/wp/2017/01/10/the-dangerous-myth-of-the-missing-Black-father/

albeit, cogent explanations as to why many of them are not there. In exploring one example of these myriad issues, mass incarceration highlights a key reason that Black men may not be present in the homes of Black families, disproportionately. According to the NAACP, Black people are incarcerated at a much higher rate (5X) than whites. Furthermore, one out of every six Black men are not present in daily life, outside of prison, ranging in age from 25 to 54 years old. While incarcerated, these men are vulnerable to myriad diseases, often smoke, and experience premature death. In terms of the death penalty, although Black people only make up 13% of the population, 35% of death penalty executions are Black people. Per the NAACP's Criminal Justice Fact Sheet, "African Americans are pursued, convicted, and sent to death at a disproportionally higher rate than any other race." [3]

Essentially, the issue of the presence, or lack thereof, pertaining to Black fathers in the home, is a complicated one. Some will argue "what about those who are just trifling and not taking care of their families." Admittedly, there is that too, in every race, but for Black men, there seems to be an emphasis on those who are missing, rather than those who are actively involved. At the time of this writing, I have been married to my husband for 36 years and this Black man has been an extremely active and present father, throughout the rearing of our now adult children. The value of his presence has been immeasurable, as he has actively participated in every

---

[3] NAACP. "Criminal Justice Fact Sheet," Accessed June 21, 2021. https://www.naacp.org/criminal-justice-fact-sheet/

aspect of their lives from the time when they were born, until now. This is not uncommon and is in-line with what many Black people know, based on our illustrious historical experience of family, in Africa, prior to the advent of slavery in the United States. Black marriage, Black parenting and Black love is valued and appreciated and the denigration of such is intolerable, through words and deeds of others, who fail to understand that the humanity of Black people is equivalent to that of any other race in the United States or otherwise.

Four

The Truth of the Present Black Father

Well-established Black men who have experiences in their lives that may preclude being with their children on a day-to-day basis are often written off as missing Black fathers, without clear understanding of their circumstances, as they pertain to their children. In this heartfelt interview, this prominent, Black father explains the in-depth, loving relationship that he has with his two young boys and the great effort he makes to ensure every moment spent with them is cherished, quality time, which does not diminish the love that he has for them. The interview is poignant as he shares his own childhood experience, in terms of his biological father, and how although it was far from perfect, it served to inspire him to be the best father possible. He is a colleague whom I have known for many years, but it was not until this interview that I learned some of the details that he shared about his life and the depth of his beautiful relationship with his children. I hope that this interview touches your heart as much as it did mine. It further clarified for me, why society needs to look at Black men from a positive lens, as fathers, rather than the broad, stereotypical brush that is often painted regarding their absence at times, from their children's lives.

Anthony (Tony) E. Munroe

Anthony E. Munroe was appointed as the Borough of Manhattan Community College's (BMCC's) 11th President and began his leadership role on September 1, 2020. He was previously President of Malcolm X College, part of the City Colleges of Chicago system. He is a first-generation U.S. citizen who grew up in the Bronx and attended New York City public schools. Tony holds a Doctorate in education from Columbia University Teachers College. His extensive experience includes serving as Associate Vice President of Health Systems Affairs at Ross University School of Medicine in New Jersey and as President of Advocate Trinity Hospital in

THE TRUTH OF THE PRESENT BLACK FATHER

Chicago. He was recently named a winner of the 2020 Phi Theta Kappa Honor Society's Paragon Award for New Presidents. Tony established the President's Fund for Excellence and Innovation at BMCC, following a $30 million gift presented to BMCC by a philanthropist.

Ari'el Munroe, Dr. Anthony Munroe and Rafa'el Munroe

Rose Trueheart: How many children do you have?

Tony: I am blessed to have two amazing, caring boys.

A RETURN TO BLACK LOVE

Rose Trueheart: How old are they?

Tony: Ari'el is 10 and his name is Hebrew for Lion of God and Rafa'el is 7 and his name is Hebrew for God is my healer.

Rose Trueheart: They are adorable. You refer to them as your heartbeats and so this is unique to you. I haven't heard anyone else that is in my circles use this term to describe their children. Can you tell me what you mean by that when you say they are your heartbeats?

Tony: They are why I exist. They are why I do what I do. It goes back to recognizing how God has blessed me so much and the greatest blessings to date has been these two boys and the awesome responsibility that has been bestowed upon me through this blessing of being their dad. They bring me joy, they are creative, they are caring. They are energetic. They are children of God. They love the Lord. They are prayer warriors. They are best friends and they are the energy that keeps me doing what I do. So that is part of what I mean when I say that they are my heartbeat, because without them, I would be lost in terms of my existence.

THE TRUTH OF THE PRESENT BLACK FATHER

Rose Trueheart: That is beautiful. As a Black father, do you think there are any unique parenting skills that are required in rearing your children?

Tony: Oh, absolutely. I think it is important, especially as a Black father of two Black boys, to not only continue to protect them, but to prepare them for the society in which we live, that no other can do. It is not theoretical for us. We have lived experiences. I have lived experiences where I have been pulled over while going to school here in New York City by the New York City Police Department. I have been racially profiled. I have been chased in the Bronx, while riding a bicycle going to work at McDonald's, by a car full of white boys and called the N word. "We are going to get you. We are going to kill you." I have cousins who have been attacked and chased in the Bronx, by white people, because of the color of their skin. Those lived experiences, as much as we do not want our children to have to grapple with it, the reality is that they will more than likely know someone and hopefully they will never have that experience. I believe very strongly that Black fathers are best positioned and best equipped for preparing their children for what this society continues to perpetrate against Black boys in particular. Even in the educational system, and being their greatest advocate, and my boys are brilliant, but even with that, ensuring that they have the best educational opportunities, the best extracurricular opportunities, that they are treated fairly and that they are not singled out and mistreated because of their appearance.

Rose Trueheart: Your boys are quite young. Do you talk to them now about these things or is this something you plan to talk to them about later?

Tony: We talk about race because their mom is of mixed race. Their maternal grandmother is a Caucasian woman, who they are around quite often, so they understand the difference in race. And they, in their minds, know that there is a difference and so we have had age appropriate conversations, and the context that has been used is that God has created us in his image, and that we are all his children and we are all equal. We recently had a conversation with my oldest about the late Reverend Dr.

THE TRUTH OF THE PRESENT BLACK FATHER

Martin Luther King and civil rights. He is old enough to get on the internet and do some research, so we talked about that. He went ahead and he did some research and found out about his most famous speech. He found out about the March on Washington, and why we have a holiday. So, these are teachable moments. I believe it is important, as a Black father, to guide your children, especially your sons, through these types of conversations, discussion and discovery. We have had those conversations, but we have not had the conversation yet around what do you do when you are in that situation, when you are racially profiled?

Rose Trueheart: Right, because they are quite young, but that conversation will come?

Tony: I think they are too young, but that conversation will come.

Rose Trueheart: For sure. Ok. Do you think it is important to spend time with your children and to be a constant presence in their lives? Now I know that is the case for you. But what is the importance behind doing that for you, as their father? Do you think it is necessary because as I explore the research and find this notion of the missing Black father, it is important to try to understand if it is necessary, from your vantage point, for the father to be a constant presence? How does that pan out in your mind for you and your sons?

Tony: I think it is important for fathers to be a strong presence and there are life situations, which will have an impact on what that looks like. What do we mean by constant? Because of our circumstances, I am not with my boys as much as I would like. They are with their mom. But I make sure that I see them every single month, for at least about a week, at least. And that consistency is critically important. As you are posing the question, I immediately recall a conversation that I had that was prompted by my oldest son, who said to me, "daddy, anytime we are with you, I feel very safe." And he went on to share some other things about how he feels deeply connected with me. He always wants to know where I am and how am I doing? My youngest is the first to offer me anything, including hugs and kisses. He will take food from his plate and offer it. So that presence, I believe needs to be a strong presence with more focus on the experience and the interaction and the quality of interaction as opposed to the quantity of time.

Rose Trueheart: Right. Also, it is important how you define constant. I think the word that I heard from you rather than constant is consistency. Is that correct?

Tony: Yes, consistency. They need to know that this is my time with my daddy and it is going to happen between this time and that time, and that is our sacred time. They shouldn't be in a position that they have to wonder and guess. Where is my daddy and when next am I going to see him?

Rose Trueheart: Okay. When you are with your children, in terms of quality time, if you could give a couple of examples, what do you do with them?

Tony: We read, we have conversations, we play games and we go on many excursions. We go on little trips, we have pillow fights, you know, we do a number of things.

Rose Trueheart: That is really important to hear, because I think there is a misunderstanding of the Black father's relationship with his children. Seemingly, it is just like everyone else. But this needs to be explained. Because as you pour through the literature, you will find that it is felt, for the most part, that these kinds of things that you are describing, are not happening. Although it seems simplistic, it is very important for us to understand that the same dynamics in terms of play, reading and conversation, and all of those things are happening.

Tony: Along those lines. I think it is important to share that I brought them, pre-COVID numerous times, to my office to see me in action. Even now, during COVID, I have shown them I am on a Zoom meeting. I have explained to them, what I do and why what I do is important so they get it. I recall last year when they were in my office, and one of my staff came into the office and introduced himself to them and my boys introduced themselves. They are very polite, and mannerly in that regard, and this staff person said, "so what do you do here?" And my youngest, my seven-year-old (he was six at that time) said my daddy is the President and we are the co-presidents and our responsibility is to take care of him. He wrote his name and his brother's name on yellow post-it notes and he put it on my office door underneath my name. I taped it to the door. Those post-it notes with their names as co-Presidents stayed on my office door. They saw it every time they visited my office. When I left my former employer, I took those same post it notes with me and they are sitting in my home office, posted up so that they could see them. When they were here last, they saw it, and my little one said "daddy you still have those" and I said yes baby because remember, and before I could even finish the sentence, he said, "yeah, we are your co-Presidents, and we are here to take care of you."

Rose Trueheart: Out of the mouths of babes... It is just too much sometimes correct? That is fantastic! Okay, well, I love that. Let's go on to the next one, which gets into a little bit more of the minutiae but the question is, were you involved with their lives when they were babies, including changing diapers, feedings all of those kinds of things? Were you hands on in that way?

Tony: Yes. Even during the pregnancy. Things happened when my oldest was born and he was in the neonatal intensive care unit for two weeks. So, I was the caregiver. I took him to his first pediatrician visit. I made all the doctor's appointments. I took care of the feedings, diaper changes, the household, everything. That was for like, six months or so. We have an exceptionally strong and different bond meaning me and my oldest. He would fall asleep on my chest. Same with my youngest. So yes, very much involved--diaper changes, going to Babies R Us and picking up formula and diapers and baby clothes and the whole nine yards; taking them to doctor's visits and then when they got to school age, taking them to school, attending school events, every week, worship service at their school and picking them up from school.

Rose Trueheart: Okay, so the answer to that is a definitive yes. The fact that you actually knew the name of the store Babies R US and so forth, I think that is pretty good. It is fantastic to know that you were so hands on with the babies because that is an area again of mystery, for some, in terms of Black men and how much participation there is in the early lives of their children.

THE TRUTH OF THE PRESENT BLACK FATHER

Tony: I had my own diaper bag and the baby bundle thing. I very rarely used it, but yeah.

Rose Trueheart: I just want you to know that if you had your own diaper bag, that is serious. Black men are often referred to as missing Black fathers. So often we hear that, correct? When you hear the term missing Black fathers, what are your thoughts? Is it true, in general, as a Black man, what is your response to that?

Tony: I think it depends on your experience because, my biological dad, I did not get to meet him until I was 18 years old. I knew his name. I knew I had older brothers and sisters, but I did not know him until I was 18 years old. After asking my mom over another year, what's the deal? What's going on? Why is my last name different? So, I experienced and have gone through the trauma and the heartache of not having my father around. I had a stepfather. I grew up saying to myself, and committing to myself that I would never do that to my children, if I ever have them, what was done to me.

Rose Trueheart: You know, it is very interesting because you and I have never talked about that. My dad was a

63

Surgeon, a Columbia College of Physicians and Surgeons graduate, but surprisingly, I did not meet my father, in person, until I was a young adult. Isn't that something? He was always present in our lives, financially, and so forth and he is a Black man. But I, too, was in the same situation, without a stepfather present. I wish you and I had known that about each other previously, because we could have commiserated.

Tony: The healing…that is, trauma. Growing up in my mind, I came up with this story that oh my dad was in the war, because no one else was telling me anything else. All I knew was my maternal grandfather, and I had all these uncles and cousins and I knew I had siblings out there but I did not know where they were or who they were. As a child, you are wondering, what's going on and what's wrong with me? Why is my dad not around? My uncles are around and interacting with my cousins, their children. Well, where's my dad? So, going back to your question, it depends on the perspective. Considering what I have been going through the last couple to three years with this divorce, the courts are not favorable to fathers. That is a whole other book.

Rose Trueheart: Yeah. And no matter what your situation is, it does not matter. Even with your level of prominence, it does not matter at all.

Tony: Exactly and I have seen that firsthand. I can understand why some have thrown their hands up and said whatever, because: A) They cannot afford it, or B) The way that the decisions are made it is not supportive and favorable towards fathers. So, my answer to that is kind of mixed. But then on the positive side, I have seen and I know because I could give you chapter and verse, of fathers who are very much active, very much present, very much in the lives of their children and dispel the stereotype that Black fathers, in particular, are missing. That story does not get told.

Rose Trueheart: Do you think that one of the reasons that there is this myth of the missing Black father is because we are not willing to share because there is a certain degree of shame associated with it? Like you said, you would say, "Well, where's my father" and so forth.

A RETURN TO BLACK LOVE

We bottle that up and we never tell that story because in my case, as I said, although my father was not present physically, he was completely in our lives. I mean, completely in terms of financial support. But, because he was missing in the eyes of everyone else, it put me in a very awkward position because of who he was. I would say that financially it was out of the ordinary, the kind of experience that I was having, without explanation. I could not explain it. So, there was a shame associated with it like when Christmas time came, and I had everything and the kids were like, well, how did you get all of that (new bicycles, clothing, toys galore, etc.), and I did not really have a way of explaining it that made sense to anyone. I walked around with that. But, I have decided after some deliberation, that I need to tell some of my story, because keeping it hidden, is not helping others to understand what happens with Black men. Right?

Tony: Right and I totally get it. And while the financial piece was not there, in my case, I am thankful that I had the opportunity to meet my dad. We have a relationship but it is not a warm, fuzzy father son relationship that one would normally expect and out of all of his children, I look the most like him.

Rose Trueheart: Isn't that something? You see, there is God, right?

Tony: I met him when I was 18 years old, at Penn Station in New York City, at a bar in New York City. Okay. Go figure. He was in New York City all this time in Brooklyn. All this time, while I was growing up in the Bronx. At some point in time, he was working in the Bronx. He was working at Bronx Lebanon hospital.

Rose Trueheart: Wow. Yeah. It was a different time. This is why these stories need to be shared because you can build up a certain degree of animosity, and you have to find forgiveness for this. But then, when you find out, at least in my case, why, and the rationale for it, and so forth… My father passed away recently, years ago, but not when I was young. He passed away, from cancer. I, for such a long time, did not understand the decision making of these two people, my mother and father. But once I understood what transpired, I had nothing but forgiveness and love for them, because it was a different time. It was a very different time. We do things a little bit differently now and they had to make decisions based on the circumstances that they were in. My mother was amazing under those circumstances, so I am so grateful for her strength and for raising me with such care.

Tony: Thank you for sharing that. Yeah and I do not think I am holding any animosity, because I do recognize a very different time, very different set of circumstances, a very different era, but that lived experience for me, got me to the place to say that, if I am blessed to be a father, I am going to be the very best father that I can be and not, not do what was done to me. I am going to break, and in fact, I am going to destroy this cycle.

Rose Trueheart: Right. That is what we must do. That is one of the reasons for this work because it is time for us to destroy these myths, and really get into what happened because there are explanations. It is not this blanket across the board, that Black fathers are just missing. My husband Jeff is the same. He did not meet his biological father until our honeymoon and the same thing happened to him. He was raised by someone else, a loving Black man, for his whole life. He thought that person was his biological father. Right before we left for our honeymoon, he found out that his adopted father that he had always thought was his biological father was not, and his biological father turned out to be the President of a college in the northeast. He is a brilliant Black man and the first Black President of that college, which is now a university. We have subsequently changed our last names to Jeff's biological father's last name. It is extremely dramatic and traumatic, what we have been through. It is not always lower income/poor, Black men in these circumstances. These are Black men of great prominence, in these two examples, that also had to make this kind of decision. So, I am glad you shared that with me. I am going to move us forward now. Do you think that history lineage and legacy is important in terms of the lives of Black children and their fathers?

Tony: Absolutely and culture is important. My roots are in the Caribbean, the West Indies. Because both of my parents, biological, were born and raised in Jamaica, I am a Jamaican citizen. I have dual citizenship, by descent.

A RETURN TO BLACK LOVE

When my children were born, I got them Jamaican citizenship.

Rose Trueheart: Excellent.

Tony: They too have dual citizenship and have the same rights as if they were born in Jamaica. So, to answer your question, yes, and I put action behind it. They are going to understand their roots. My oldest Ari'el says that his favorite music is Calypso.

Rose Trueheart: So, he is in touch with the roots.

Tony: Very much so. That is part of legacy. I am now slowly and gently teaching them about self-empowered social systems like my fraternity. My son asked "What is Alpha Phi Alpha? I told him, if you decide to become a member, this is why Alpha was created. This is what Alpha stands for. So, yes, that is important.

Rose Trueheart: In terms of financial legacy, do you think that is important? Because in the Black community, one of the things that becomes very important is making sure that we are not just thinking about this generation, but the generations going forward. What are your thoughts in terms of legacy and financial matters. Do you think that is valid and something to prepare for?

Tony: Absolutely because everything that I have, will be and is already in their name. The 529, the 401k whatever it is, it is all for them. The insurance policies that I have. It is all for them.

Rose Trueheart: That is fantastic! Given your active parenting role in the lives of your children, what advice do you have for young Black men regarding fatherhood and their futures?

Tony: It is a tremendous blessing, an honor and a privilege to be protected and valued. It is sacred and it is not a transaction. Someone wise once said to me "you never know that love of a parent until you become a parent."

Rose Trueheart: That is for sure.

Tony: Until you have experienced becoming a father, becoming a mother, becoming a parent, you really do not have a full understanding and appreciation of the sanctity of that relationship, that connection, that bond. I can tell you this. There is nothing that I would not do for my children. Without any hesitation, I would lay my life down for both of my children. No if, ands, and buts about it. And understanding that as a young dad is ultimate, unconditional love. And I tell my children, they could be anything that they want and always know that daddy is always here. I may not be here, physically, but I am with you. I am always thinking about you and I will always love you.

Rose Trueheart: Right. And that cannot be taken for granted as if they assume that to be the case. It has to be said to them.

Tony: It has to be said to them and you have to demonstrate that to them as well. Love is not just giving them things. Love is giving of yourself, giving of your time, sharing experiences with them, comforting them, making them feel safe, making them feel heard and valued and demonstrating to them how proud you are of them and celebrating them.

Rose Trueheart: Absolutely. I agree. Do you think that education is important for Black fathers? If so, why? And if not, why?

THE TRUTH OF THE PRESENT BLACK FATHER

Tony: Oh, absolutely. There is formal educational and informal education. Every opportunity to learn and grow is critically important. I think as a Black father, as a Black male, education is absolutely key because we know that the more you learn, the more earning potential you have and if we want economic mobility, that really rests primarily on your education and your training. Right? And I believe I am an example of that. What I earn today, not just because of my years of being out in the field, is very different from what I earned when I had a high school diploma or when I had a Bachelor's degree or Master's degree. So yes, I totally believe, and not just because I am in education as a profession now, but I see the payoff for having an education and I want my children to have that. In fact, we talk about graduating from college and going on. Just the other day my boys were saying, I do not know if I want to become a doctor because I do not want to be called doctor. You are Doctor Munroe. I had to think about that and I explained to them that there are different types of doctors and not everyone is a medical doctor. Medical doctors take care

73

of people and deliver babies, but then you have other others who earn a doctoral degree in a particular discipline and they are called doctors. "Oh, yeah, I can do that," one of them said. I just want to open up this whole world of conversation about the importance of education. Instilling that in them at this young age, I think is critically important. And so, yes, education for Black fathers, in particular, I think is absolutely, essential.

Rose Trueheart: The question that I want to piggyback on here is, for those men, young Black men, not really young, but just Black men in general, who, for whatever reason, did not get the education and are not pursuing it for whatever reason, what advice would you give them in terms of fatherhood? Because we do have to understand that not all Black men, for whatever reason, and sometimes it is reasons beyond their control, or they just did not do it or whatever, they are not educated, but yet, they are still fathers. What is your advice to those Black men?

Tony: Well, we know that not everyone is going to be able to pursue and get a college education. Not everyone is cut out for that and not everyone's circumstances will allow for that. That is okay. But, find a way to get maybe some trade/training certificate, an ability to take care of yourself and your family, your children, your obligations.

Rose Trueheart: That is very good advice. I know, as educators, that is a tough question to deal with. But it is a real question, because we actually have to address this issue in the Black community. We cannot leave those individuals out that it does not happen for. But at the same time, we still have to impress upon them, you have to do something, though.

Tony: To put it into context, Black women are outpacing Black men in college education. In fact, today, in many educational institutions, Black women outnumber Black men. Now, there are different reasons for that, but the ability is there. The ability, and in many cases, the opportunity is there to continue to encourage it and to support it, and make it happen.

Rose Trueheart: Do you have any words of wisdom to share about being a Black father? And how does it feel?

A RETURN TO BLACK LOVE

Tony: Just continue to reflect on how blessed you are to be called daddy or dad. It is an awesome blessing to be a father, whether it is your biological child or not. Being a father figure and experiencing that love, that responsibility is awesome and is never to be squandered or taken advantage of. Someone wise also said to me, "the days may be long but the years are short."

Rose Trueheart: That is so true. Maximize every moment with your children. Be present, not just physically, but be present in every dimension possible. Okay, definitely words of wisdom there. Let's go to your feelings for a moment. How does it feel to be with your children?

Tony: It is life giving for me. I can share that there are many times when I have cried because I am yearning to see my children. I cherish those moments. Just to be in their presence gives me life, energy and joy.

Rose Trueheart: Well, that is wonderful. Thank you so much.

Tony: Thank you for the invitation.

Five

Ghanaian vs. Black American Families

Recently, I mentioned to a colleague, Annie Daniel, PhD, that I was interested in exploring, comparatively, the lives of Black people in the United States as compared to those in Ghana as many Black people in the Americas are from this particular part of West Africa, as a result of the transatlantic slave trade. She informed me that she had conducted research on this topic, as she spent time studying abroad in Ghana, Africa. Consequently, she shared that detail with me, which is provided in this chapter. Exploring this information, in a brief, largely outline format, provides a context, for Black people living in the United States, to understand the family structure, in a very significantly relevant country (Ghana), for Black people in the U.S., since it is in West Africa. It provides context, which may be useful in trying to understand our ways as Black people, as we live and thrive in the United

States, which for many is home. There is also an opportunity to understand differences, because undoubtedly, being born and raised in the U.S. is quite different, in terms of culture, than living in Ghana, but nevertheless, upon a closer look, some of the similarities are quite apparent.

<u>**Ghanaians**</u>
Strong kinship bonds

> A favorable attitude towards the elderly
> Adaptability of family roles
> Strong work/achievement orientation

Family Characteristics

> Types of families:

> > The nuclear family
> > The polygamous family
> > The extended family

The extended family plays a role in social control by putting pressure on individuals to conform to accepted ways of behavior. A large proportion of households are headed by women in Accra, Ghana. Accra is the capital city. Female-headed households tend to constitute a large proportion of small households consisting of two to four persons. Traditionally, men and women in Ghana lived separately, even after marriage. The proportion of more distant relatives sheltering within the household is greater in female-headed households than in male-headed households. Male-headed households tend to have higher levels of education than female-headed households. The age of marriage has been set at 18, eliminating the traditional marriages at ages as low as 12. Children are traditionally raised in the mother's house, with male children going to live with their fathers at about the age of ten. Going as far back as 1995, 64% of Ghana's population was literate. Women have a lower literacy rate than men. Foreign content of the school syllabus alienated the Ghanaians from traditional environment and culture, thus graduates knew more about European culture than their own culture. Migration to larger cities is common, where the jobs are abundant .

Factors Which Impacted the Ghanaian Family Structure

<u>Colonialism</u> - Brought foreign political, economic and social environments that did not exist before colonial rule.

<u>Christianity</u>- Brought the Bible and book knowledge to woo converts.

<u>Money-using economy</u> - In pre-colonial days, most Africans, Ghanaians included, used other currencies such as cowries, gold dust, iron and brass as mediums of exchange.

<u>Formal classroom education</u>- Forced adoption to European life-styles, such as types of attire, food choices, music and dancing among other habits.

Colonialism also led to the introduction of individualism and weakening of the traditional authority structure and kinship ties. Parental socialization of the child was also introduced. School age children now spend more time with their teachers and peers than with their parents, thus reducing the parents' role in the children's socialization process.

GHANAIAN VS. BLACK AMERICAN FAMILIES

Urbanization

Unlike the traditional setting, urban areas are characterized by life-styles of impersonal behavior, anonymity, secularism and elimination of kinship ties. The major factors of change, including colonialism, a money-using economy and formal classroom education have all encouraged migration from rural areas into the large towns and employment centers.

<u>African Americans</u>

Family Characteristics

Types of families:

The nuclear family (including blended and single-headed)

The extended family

African American Family Characteristics

Extended family members give care, support and strength.

Grandparents, in some cases, will raise their grandchildren.

A RETURN TO BLACK LOVE

In urban areas, a large percentage of the
households are female-headed.
A significant portion of African Americans live in
metropolitan areas.

Factors of Change in the African American Family

The Transatlantic Slave Trade had a devastating effect
on African American family life. Below are some of the
unfortunate outcomes:

Destroyed family pattern and structure.

Customs regarding marriage, sexuality,
socialization, religious rites and family obligations
were forbidden.

A preponderance of single-headed (mothers)
families, out-of-wedlock births, and social
immobility developed.

Substantial poverty exists in largely segregated
communities with limited resources. Post slavery,
emancipation helped with reforming families, male

suffrage, rights of citizenship and the allowance of freedom of movement. The subsequent sharecropping system was exploited as white people overcharged Black people for use of land, housing, food and other materials. Overall, it boils down to economic ills experienced by Black people, post-slavery. Economic deprivation threatens the stability of extended family networks and of conjugal and parental relations. The low economic status of Black males affects marriage ability and racism affects the young and old, the poor and the middle class. Racism led to, and continues to lead to economic hardships, even for Black people who experience higher education and often results in exploitation in the labor market.

Summary

There are seven common strengths that exist in both African American and Ghanaian families, which are: (1) strong kinship bonds, (2) a favorable attitude toward the elderly, (3) adaptability of family roles, (4) strong work/achievement orientation, (5) love of children, (6) resilience/continued ability to survive and (7) strong religious orientation. Additionally, there are several similarities between African American and Ghanaian families in the following areas:

> Urban family structure;
> Urban family patterns
> Factors that caused change in the families (colonialism and slavery)

Ultimately, with the exception of slavery vs. colonization, and racism vs. tribalism among the African American and Ghanaian families respectively, the differences that exist between the two, in terms of family, are minimal.

Exercise

Family Structure

Sit in a quiet space where you can reflect on your family, from childhood to early adulthood.

Write down your answers to these questions:

> Who was the head of household in your family?

GHANAIAN VS. BLACK AMERICAN FAMILIES

Was your mother and your father present and if not, why not, if either of them were missing?

Did you have grandparents on your maternal and paternal side?

Did your grandparents live in your home/nearby?

What was your favorite food growing up and who did most of the cooking in your home?

Describe the house(s)/living space(s), that you grew up in, with detail.

Did your family move often or did you live in the same house throughout your childhood?

How did your financial situation feel (poor, rich or something in-between)?

Who provided for your family financially (your mother, your father or both)?

Were your parents educated below or beyond high school? Your mother? Your father?

Was your family religious?

A RETURN TO BLACK LOVE

Was education emphasized, for you, by your parents?

Did you like school and did you do well, poorly or something in between?

Did you travel outside of the country with your family?

Have you ever visited West Africa?

Reflect on your answers to these questions and determine if they mean anything to you, in terms of your overall story and who and what you are today. Do you see similarities between your experience and some of the details pertaining to Ghana above? As African Americans, Black people living in America, sometimes connections are not made to our African lineage at all. In fact, there are some Black people who deny their African lineage and are perhaps offended when asked to consider this because they identify as wholly American. Or perhaps, one may identify solely with their Caribbean heritage, as an example, even if they are born and raised in the United

GHANAIAN VS. BLACK AMERICAN FAMILIES

States. This is perfectly understandable, for one to identify solely with the place that they were born and raised, but the acknowledgement of the fact that Africa is the original home of the ancestors of Black people, no matter where they are, goes a long way towards understanding ourselves on a deeper level. Sometimes, it is hard to imagine how to make that connection, especially if you have never been to Africa, especially West Africa, but it is real, The connection was interrupted, by slavery, and there are undeniable similarities between Black people on either side of the Atlantic ocean.

Six

In It 100 Percent

I was a graduate student at Yale University, out for an evening of just hanging out with one of my classmates, another Black woman. We were young, in our early twenties, basically single and on that evening, we vowed that we were not looking to meet any guys. There we sat, at a local music spot and eatery when in walked a group of guys. One was especially fine, as pointed out to me by my friend. I jokingly reminded her that we were not out to meet guys, and as we listened to music, I got up to go and play pinball in the back area. I was certain that my casual attire of jeans, an off-white, basic sweater, short flat boots and little to no make-up would preclude any interest in me, by any guy, as modesty was my choice that night. As I played pinball, I heard someone say hello to me. I turned around and it was him, standing behind me. We chatted and talked for the rest of the evening as he joined us at our table with his roommate (they were both

IN IT 100 PERCENT

Yale students, too), a short Italian guy, whom my friend was definitely not interested in, but she was politely talking with him. That handsome Black guy, who approached me at the pinball machine, walked us to our dorm later that evening. We talked all the way there, and the two of us talked longer, and we finally said goodbye. He was a gentleman, smart, handsome, kind, friendly and from that evening forward, we were rarely apart again. After nearly 36 plus years of marriage and two children (a girl and a boy, now grown and a Professor and a Lawyer whom we love and are so proud of and adore both of them) we remain together, immersed in Black love. I truly enjoyed interviewing and listening to my husband talk about our love, our family, and our journey through this life together.

Jeffrey Rose Trueheart

Jeffrey Rose Trueheart, born and raised in Norwich, Connecticut, graduated from Yale University with a B.A. in Economics and Political Science. He held corporate finance positions before transitioning into healthcare financial roles. He served as the Assistant Director of Finance at a NYC and Florida Hospital and as the Director of Finance for a multi-institution health concern in Florida. Jeffrey left healthcare finance and began a career in education at a private, independent, Episcopal school in Florida. Since that time, he has taught courses in mathematics and Finance at both the middle and high school levels at a this private, and for a brief time, at a large, public high school, before returning to a private school. In addition to his teaching responsibilities, Jeff also has spent numerous years coaching varsity baseball, basketball, and golf, served as an Academic Coach for other Teachers at a public school, and served for four years as the Assistant Director of Athletics there. He served for three years as the Director of Athletics at the private school, where he currently works. He views his move into education as his true calling and the perfect method for him to provide service to others. He has been happily married for more than 36 years and is the proud father of one daughter, (a University Professor) and one son (an Attorney), currently serving as a General Counsel for an international company.

Then…

Jeff, Courtney, Patti and Brandon
and recently…

Brandon, Patti, Courtney and Jeff
Ghana (Year of Return Trip, Summer 2019)

A RETURN TO BLACK LOVE

Rose Trueheart: How long have you been married?

Jeff: Thirty-six years plus.

Rose Trueheart: Okay, and how did you meet?

Jeff: We met when I was in college. We were both Yale students and you were in graduate school. We met at Toad's Place in New Haven, Connecticut.

Rose Trueheart: For the sake of the reader, what is Toad's Place?

Jeff: Toads place is a bar/music venue with live music. Bands would come out to try out their music before they went to New York or Boston, to go on tour.

Rose Trueheart: Where is Toads Place located?

Jeff: It is right in the midst of the Yale campus area. It was only steps away from my dormitory, Ezra Stiles.

Rose Trueheart: So, you mentioned Yale. Tell me more about how it relates to your story. Would you say college sweethearts is applicable?

Jeff: Yes. For sure. We were Yale students.

Rose Trueheart: Alright. Did you consciously choose to marry a Black woman? And if so, why?

IN IT 100 PERCENT

Jeff: Absolutely. Without a doubt. There was never a question. It is all I ever knew. It was never something that was consciously talked about. For me, just looking around, everybody I knew was married to a person of color. I knew I was going to marry a woman of color. It was not even a question, but just what was supposed to happen.

Rose Trueheart: Specifically, you use the term woman of color. Are you referring to Black women? When you say every person I knew was married to another person of color? Do you mean every Black person you knew was married to another Black person?

Jeff: Yes. I only mean Black people. There was not anyone from any other background. So, yeah, Black people.

Rose Trueheart: I happen to know that when you refer to Black people in your family, you are referring to a particular nationality of Black people. Would you just go over that just a little bit?

Jeff Sure. So, everyone in my family, in the area where I was raised, because it turned out that I found out more things about my biological father later, but everyone in the family, that I understood to be my family, was of Cape Verdean descent. The Cape Verde islands are just off of the west coast of Africa. These islands are considered an African nation. The inhabitants are African, mainly Senegalese, mixed with Portuguese. The Portuguese came and took over the islands and made them a colony until 1975. This was confusing, I think, when I was really young, because many of the Cape Verdean people in the United States, or at least in the areas of Connecticut and Massachusetts, where I grew up, identified as Cape Verdean, not as Black. So, that was kind of weird, but they are Black. There were people who were native to the island, that is probably a small population, and then escaped slaves. Then the Portuguese arrived.

Rose Trueheart: Very interesting. We have been married for a long time, 36 years, and counting, as you have said, and so the question is, what do you attribute to the longevity of our union? Give me a couple of key factors from your vantage point?

IN IT 100 PERCENT

Jeff: Well, I think the first thing is that we really communicate well with each other. That was something that personally, I had to improve upon. I was not raised in a very communicative family environment. It was kind of quiet. There was talking but there was not a lot of expression. I had to learn to become a little more open and do those things. But having learned that, it is easy to see that it is key. It is been a key force in helping us stay together, because we always are clear with each other. There are no gray areas. You do not have to guess. So that is one thing. I think both of us remain very, very committed to ourselves, to each other, to our family, to the children and to all of our dreams and aspirations. I do not know why I was blessed this way, but clearly I am blessed. I am blessed by having a person placed into my life, that is just right; a perfect match for me, in every way, shape and form. We are Yin and Yang. However, you want to talk about it, I cannot even visualize life without you.

Rose Trueheart: That is so beautiful. I am deeply touched. So, for the latter part of your response, would you say that is how you would describe love? As you know, this book is about Black love. The last factor that you mentioned, the perfect match. Would that be how you describe love in terms of our relationship?

Jeff: Yes, but, I think love is so much bigger than that. That is part of it, maybe the early initial way that we got together and started to develop. It is caring about each other and being willing to do whatever is necessary to make sure that the other person feels supported, loved, cared for, thought about. It is about being grateful for them. I feel that the person is grateful to have the other person in their life. I mean, I think in this society and the world, Black love is different. It is different because of the challenges that we face as Black people just trying to live our lives, unlike what other people face. You have to be willing to take on those challenges as an individual and as a couple. I think that is where true love is really born. That unity of being in this struggle together, no matter what. That is Black love.

Rose Trueheart: That was great. We have two children, ages 34 and 36, which is shocking to many, including us.

IN IT 100 PERCENT

We raised these two, now adults, together, and we are very proud of them. As a Black father, do you think that there any unique aspects in your approach to parenting?

Jeff: Sure. It goes along with what I said previously. Black fathers and Black mothers do not have the luxury of just being able to parent their children along basic lines of information. You cannot just say, do what is right and, and be a moral, high character person and let them go out into the world and not really be concerned about them because Black children, as they are being raised, face a different set of circumstances than their white counterparts, especially here, given the history of this country, and slavery and all that entailed. I think, having gone through childhood myself and the different challenges that I faced, growing up as a Black child and becoming a man, by the time I was able and blessed to have children, I knew I had to pass on a lot of those survival skills to both of our children, Brandon, a Black man and Courtney, a Black woman. So, yeah, I think there are distinct differences and things that I had to pay attention to as a Black father that are different from my white counterparts.

Rose Trueheart: You have been very active in their lives. Please share two examples of how.

Jeff: Yeah, I have been pretty active. We can use the example of our daughter when she was really young. We were living in Manchester, Connecticut, and I was actually the stay at home dad for a short period of time. You were working a new position and I was not working as I was planning on going back to school for a graduate degree. But, in the interim, before that could happen, I was at home and I was literally the stay at home Dad, taking care of the kids, feeding them and making sure Courtney was ready for dance school in Hartford, CT. I went to every single one of her rehearsals, practices, and whatever. Beyond that brief experience, throughout her life, I filmed all of her shows, from when she was tiny in dancing school all the way up through when she was in the marching band in high school.

Rose Trueheart: Yes. So true. During much of that time, besides your short stay at home dad time, you were

IN IT 100 PERCENT

working 50 hours per week in the area of Hospital
Finance. It amazed me how hard you worked and how
attentive you were, also, to the children's experiences.
Can you give me one more example of how you were
actively involved in the lives of the kids?

Jeff: Everything that we did, I was actively involved. But,
there was nothing, that either of the children did that I
was not actively involved in. If I could not be there,
which was rare, I would discuss with them what
happened and hear all the stories about them. When I was
working in New York, and we lived in Connecticut, I
could not be involved with their day to day school
experience because I was at work and had a two-hour
commute, driving each way. I would always get the full
rundown when I got home or talk to you and them by
phone. I cannot think of any activity or any incident, on
any day, that something happened that I was not involved
in. There was quite a bit of athletics, too. That was one of
the huge connections for Brandon and me because we
both really love athletics and are passionate about them.
It is the same way that my father and uncles taught me

everything that I knew, about different sports, and how to play them, how to appreciate them and how to carry myself. I did the same thing with Brandon. I was integrally involved with all of his athletic endeavors and academically with both kids. I mean, academically, it is obviously something that is really important to both of us, making sure that we were enriching our minds all the time. It was critically important that we were raising children who were passionate about learning. We desired information and knew how to go get it and so education was always the priority for us. We were very, integrally involved in their education, including making visits to school whenever necessary to keep people straight.

Rose Trueheart: Yes, for sure! Also, as a Black father, do you think that history, lineage and legacy are important in terms of your family? And if so how?

Jeff: Yes, absolutely, because there is nothing else. We all have a set amount of time here on the planet, whatever that is. We do not know how long that is. But whenever that time comes to its end, the only thing that you leave behind is your history of how you carried yourself and the legacy of your family. That is what carries forward. You are no longer here, physically but your history and your legacy carries forward. It kind of keeps you alive. My grandfather, uncles, and aunts, mother, father and everyone who has passed their legacy lives on through how I carry myself and how I live my life, not only in name, but in action. It is critically important to me, for Courtney and Brandon, to carry on all of that, plus any and everything that they add through their families and children to come.

Rose Trueheart: In terms of legacy, you are speaking of our children sort of being representative, after we are gone, of who we are and of themselves. Do you look at this also from a financial situation, namely financial legacy?

Jeff Rose: Of course, I mean, nothing exists here where people are able to sustain themselves on this planet, without some sort of financial wherewithal. And so, lots of time, effort and energy has been put in to building and passing along financial legacy in our family so that the people who come after have to struggle less. That was one of the reasons for emphasizing education. Like every parent, you want to place your children in a position where they are continuing to progress. My parents and grandparents did things to get me into a position where I was at a good starting point. I think that we have definitely taken that forward and raised the bar even a little bit higher. Now we are passing along to Brandon and Courtney an even better, more advantageous position to start from so that they can then take it to another level.

Rose Trueheart: Perfect. Let's talk about advice. What message would you offer to young Black men who are dating and thinking of marriage at some point in the near distant future, particularly in terms of Black women?

Jeff: Well, a couple of things. First, I do not think you can go into the dating world, searching for your wife. You cannot do that. You have to do two things. You have to be completely comfortable and happy in a way, being by yourself because if you are always searching I think that all you will ever do is search. I do not believe you find someone. I think somebody finds you. Secondly, I also think you wander into a circumstance where you are brought together with the person that you need to be with. Too many people are always searching and they never find. You have to be comfortable and really clear about who you want to be with and what your expectations are. You can wander into that situation where that person is going to bump into you. You have to clearly define in your mind, what kind of person you are looking for. I think that is important. Thirdly and obviously, you have to understand the legacy of your own individual family that you are trying to create and care for, because that is important. We are also a part of a bigger legacy, right? We are part of African people that were transported here against their will, and yet somehow found ways to create, continue and expand life. We are part of that legacy. It is critically important for us to acknowledge and accept and relish our part in that legacy, so that we can do our best moving forward.

Rose Trueheart: If a young Black man is dating and he comes to you and asks for advice, besides the key things that you just said, in terms of Black women, what would you say to that young man? Is there any key advice that you think a young Black man needs, when he is dating, and thinking of marriage at some point, particularly as it relates to Black women?

Jeff: I just think if you are true and honest to yourself and in the relationship, that is what is needed. Black women are beautiful and special, but they are not a different species, right? It is not something special that you have to do, but you have to love them the way that you should love them. You have to care for them and respect them. For any young guys who are struggling, I just think you have to relax about it first, and not worry about it and know that it is not on your time, it is on God's time, in terms of finding a Black woman to love. Those are different calendars. You just have to relax and know that there is a sister out there that is right for you, and you are going to find her or rather she is going to find you. You are going to bump into each other. It is probably not going to happen the way that you think it is going to happen. I would tell the young man who seeks my advice on this to just relax.

IN IT 100 PERCENT

Rose Trueheart: Your key words on this seem to be relax and faith. Great. The next question is what are the most important aspects of marriage from your vantage point? Earlier, you talked about communication and love, but what else?

Jeff: I would say diligence. Just like anything else in life, relationships have their challenges and you have to be willing and happy to put the time and effort into it. That makes it sound like a grind but it is not. I am talking more about the mundane things. For me, as a man, I always felt that it was really important that I do whatever I could to provide financially for my family. That even meant, for a significant period of time, getting up at whatever time in the morning and driving two hours to work, and working a full day and then driving two hours home. It is those things that matter, or on the weekends, just being there and doing stuff that needs to get done. That is what I am talking about with diligence. Just be all in, all the time.

Rose Trueheart: That answer is excellent and pertains specifically to the family part. Let's talk a little bit more about marriage, because that is important. We had our children early. Having children was definitely a salient point for us, but what about marriage—the husband and wife?

Jeff Rose: I think being conscious all the time of you, what you are dealing with is really important. It goes both ways. When you are in a relationship, in a marriage, you are no longer that single person, by yourself. Getting married means, you become one person. They are still two people, but functioning as a single unit. The only way that works is if both people are conscious and aware and appreciative of their own self. Of course, you have to love yourself and not give yourself away. But simultaneously, you have to be just as conscious and aware of the other person in the relationship and what he or she is feeling, going through, needs, wants including support or whatever it is to help the other person move forward and progress. I think that is what ruins a lot of relationships. When one or both of the people become unwilling to stay connected with what the other person needs, that is a problem and they start becoming a little more selfish, and saying, well, is this what I need? I do not give a damn. I think for us, we have always stayed conscious and cognizant of the other person and being present for them and aware. I am not perfect. I make mistakes, but we are always really concerned with what the other person is going through. I am just happy to think that when you are at the point where even after more than 36 years of marriage, you are really happy, especially when you can do something that makes the other person happy. That is strong and that is love.

Rose Trueheart: All right. So that is good, because in terms of Black love, we are really trying to get to what the source is? What is it? What really makes it work? My next question is do you think, in terms of Black men, as husbands and fathers, that their educational level matters, relative to the educational status of the Black woman?

Jeff: I think definitely, because we started this conversation talking about the importance of communication. I cannot imagine ways to do so if the educational level is vastly different between the two, the husband and wife. I do not see ways where they are going to be able to communicate effectively, at all times. In a way that is beneficial to both, because whichever of the two is more educated, in the conversation, it is going to reach a point where the other person cannot really share, help and contribute. They can always say things, but, if there is a point where the conversation gets beyond your ability to understand that is a serious problem. I think what people do not come to terms with is the fact that life events do not ever stop happening. In a marriage, you are always faced with, hey, this just happened. Let us talk about it. It could be something in your house or outside that is happening, that you need to figure out how we are going to respond to it. The thing that has helped and strengthened us tremendously is the fact that I know I can talk about things and when I cannot talk about things or if I do not understand something fully, I can research it, find out and get more details. We have never stopped having really impressive, intelligent conversations about a myriad of things. I feel like if I hadn't gone through the educational circles that I went through, I could not have had these conversations. I know that because I have friends who have not done it, educationally, and I cannot even have in-depth conversations with them.

Rose Trueheart: Yeah, so let's talk about that for a moment, because when we met, we were both students at Yale. In our conversations, we have said this, and this is not something coming from the vantage point of an elite mindset, or anything to that effect. But, while we were students, our conversations together with other people on campus, as an example, were very profound in many instances. When we were no longer college students, we have said to each other that we find that our conversations are not the same with other people. What does that mean for you as a Black man?

Jeff: I think that, in some ways, humanity has devolved over 1000's of years. We went to Egypt and lots of different places throughout the world, but specifically Egypt, and we saw things that were created, 1000's of years ago, without computers and sophisticated tools, as we currently understand them. It really brought home the understanding, to me, that humanity, at that point, was operating mentally, at a level that was far beyond where

109

we are currently able to operate. When we roll that forward to now and into this question, and talk about Black guys here, and how their educational training or whatever fits into relationships, I just think that the one thing that is critically missing in many people, and unfortunately, it disproportionately affects Black communities, is that we are no longer trained in really just how to think. Our minds are amazing and we have the capacity to do things that we do not even understand. We do not use our minds to full capacity. When you do kind of stumble across the small percentage of people who have, for whatever reason, either been trained to understand how to think, or have a special innate ability to know how to think deeply, then you end up having those conversations you were talking about in your question. We talked about how we had those conversations in groups all around our college campuses, and we had the belief that when we leave college, we are going to continue to have these conversations. But, then you leave college and meet people in the outside world and you realize immediately, oh, I cannot have that conversation with this person because he or she is not even close in understanding how to do so. I do not want to use the word elite. I think that is the wrong word. I just think it is just people who, for whatever reason, have not been afforded the opportunity to learn how to use their God given minds, because everybody has the ability to do it. But if you are not taught how to do it, you may not be open to it.

Rose Trueheart: This is my last question. Do you have any parting thoughts about Black love and parenting? Do you have any pearls of wisdom that you want to share?

Jeff: Yes. I used to say this, and I still say it to people who are just becoming parents or just newlyweds. There have been no joys that are better than those that I have gotten from my relationships with you and my children. The relationship you have with your wife, and your children as a Black man has a level of purity that does not exist anywhere else in your life. When I would come home from work, and the kids were really small, coming home to you and them was so great and coming home to you, now that our nest is empty, is still great. Also, if I had said I was going to do something or bring something back to them, the kids would say, did you bring me this? And I would say, yeah, it is right here. The look, from Courtney or Brandon or from you, of joy and appreciation and love, was purer than anything that I had ever experienced, up to that point.

My pearls of wisdom, to anybody, especially young Black guys who are beginning relationships and starting a family, is to fully dive in. Give totally of yourself. Do not be fearful or worry. Just dive in, and be in it 100% because I promise you that if you do that, and I am not saying it is going to be easy; I am not saying you are not going to struggle with things or that there are not going to be hurdles, because they will pop up. But, you will feel the power and strength of having a Black woman by your side, and you will feel the power and strength of being a Black man inside of you. When you support or fight for what is right for your children, it is a power that I cannot even put into words. I cannot describe how strong it is and how much it lifts you up, even at times when you feel crushed and that you do not know anything. Everything says we, Black people, should not have made it in this country. I am telling you, that you, young Black guys who are starting families with a Black woman, have been blessed in a way that you cannot even begin to imagine. I know that I am. Again, be in it 100%. Go for it and the things that you will experience will be beyond your expectations.

Rose Trueheart: That was excellent! I feel loved and inspired. Thank you.

Seven

Black Love Is the Answer

If Black Love is the answer what are the questions?

> How will we survive?
>
> How have we survived?
>
> How do we continue our people, our families, and our legacy?
>
> What is our love?
>
> How do we sustain ourselves?
>
> Why are we here?
>
> What can we show the world?
>
> How can we connect to the fact that we are Africans?

The answer to these questions is indeed Black love. Black love is the endurance of pain, while simultaneously feeling joy. I have only known Black Love. My mother was Black. I knew her love. It was strong, real and bold, but without a great deal of touch, except when she bathed me, as a child, or did my hair. She was not big on hugging but I knew that she loved me at all times, based on her concern, care and being present in my life. She was a fantastic southern cook from the state of Georgia. Without exaggeration, anticipating her food and then actually eating it was one of the highlights of my life. She came to New York City, alone, during the great migration, to get away from Jim Crow laws. She said she had to leave Georgia because she was not going through back doors and experiencing other segregationist scenarios, because given her refusal to do so, adamantly, she might get harmed, physically or otherwise. My father was Black. I was never touched by him as a child, because I met him, in person, as a young adult. Perhaps he held me as a baby but I do not remember that. As a Surgeon, he felt holding me in the embrace of his money, throughout my life, was enough. It was not. However, I respect and honor him because he was my father and I told him so. I am grateful that I did so, before he left this world, in the form of a long, heartfelt letter, that he received and acknowledged. I understand that parenting is difficult, is often far from perfect but that love has the capacity to recognize the full spectrum of an individual and to try and understand them, rather than carry what is perhaps unwarranted pain and sorrow, based on misunderstanding or lack of the full picture of the person's life. In doing that, retrospectively, I have grown to embrace my father, in the spirit of Black love, appreciation, respect and with honor.

Growing up, I experienced Black love in various forms. My siblings are/were Black. One, the eldest, was my protector, for the most part, as we grew up together. She is five years older than me. The youngest, showed and continues to show love in intense ways. Her current love is and always has been generosity of spirit. She is a very kind person. The only boy, my beloved brother, presented as love, offering a tremendous amount of intelligence, wisdom beyond his years, humor and a sense of wonderment. He was my brother and a true friend. We, me and the world, lost him too soon, at the age of 31. It seems that he knew that he would not be on earth very long because his love was intense and powerful, in my life, and many who knew him felt the same. He had a fantastic sense of humor and a brilliant mind. I still hear his wittiness and laughter in my mind, when things go down in my life, that I know we would have discussed intensely. He was over six feet tall and rather thin and muscular and his laugh would fill the room with joy. In a nutshell, the people above were familial Black love in my life as I grew up. There were no other relatives of ours living in Queens, NY, which was our home. We were a close-knit, small family.

I created a list of all of the key words/phrases related to the brief synopsis of the relationship with my family, above. The list includes:

> Delicious food
> Strength
> Authenticity
> Generosity
> Smart
> Intelligence
> Humor

A RETURN TO BLACK LOVE

Happiness

Wisdom

This list is the start of an exercise, that I highly recommend, which can be repeated often as it may change, from time to time, in terms of memory/reflection about family. I have summarized the process for this Exercise below.

Exercise I

Family

Free write, in prose, about family in your early life (from childhood to early adulthood). Do not worry about grammar, spelling, length or any formal steps. Try to answer the following questions about your mother, father, siblings and any other close relatives that you had constant contact with, as you write:

How did they love you?

Did you love them?

How did love feel?

What was missing?

What stands out?

BLACK LOVE IS THE ANSWER

Ask these questions about each family member that comes to mind. Be 100% truthful. Review what you wrote and circle at least ten words that stand out or derive the words from the content. List them and read each word aloud, imaging the person (people) that the words are relevant to. Look at the words. Say them out loud more than once, so you hear them clearly. Circle all of the positive words in the list and cross out all of the negatives. The goal is to focus on the goodness of your Black love experience with your family. For those people who fled to joyous energy, close your eyes and send them love, whether they are living or dead. If the thoughts of any of the people that you wrote about brings you pain, as the musical artist Londrelle sings "Let the Trauma Go." Release their negative energy from your mind, body, soul and spirit. Send them love and release the negative energy, with a deep breath in and a deep breath out. Free your mind of any pain that may have occurred between you and one of them and think of all of your family members, in your summary, with pure love.

Exercise II

Black Mother Love

As you reflect, further, beyond the exercise above, focus on your mother and ask the following questions.

> What is/was her skin tone?
>
> What is/was her hair texture?
>
> What is/were her facial features?
>
> What is/was her body type?
>
> How did her hands feel when she touched you?

As you fixate on her physical characteristics, keep in mind that to be a Black mother and to love your Black children, in the United States, is a beautiful and daunting task. There is no perfection. Outcomes can be beautiful, in terms of accomplishments and achievements of children, but the intrinsic aspect of a Black mother's children, figuring out their way in this society, is the tricky part—especially as they become/are adults.

This society tells Black women that they have to be thin, with long, preferably straight hair or extremely curly (loose curls). Her skin has to be of a certain complexion (light preferred) or extremely dark in a stand-out way (think Lupita Nyong'o). If she is extremely dark, short cropped hair is usually preferred, in this society, in terms of preferred beauty. Black women must achieve beyond measure, educationally or otherwise, and exude success. They cannot be angry or loud and are encouraged by society, through the media, movies, and beyond, to try to be like white women as much as possible. White women have historically been presented in all forms of media (television, movies, advertisements, etc.) as the most desirous, in all walks of life, and some believe that they are, because some Black men will melt in the arms of their pursuit of them, leaving the Black woman behind, whether the Black woman is the mother of their children or not. Of course, this is generalized and seemingly stereotypical, but in some cases, not far from the truth.

Consequently, some Black women will strive to be like white women by changing their hair texture and length to resemble white women. They will try to be thin, if they are not thin naturally, and some will try to lighten their complexion with creams, make-up, etc. The white woman is the proverbial brass ring, for some Black men, in the carousel of life, so some Black women will try to be that for Black men, as the other ring that many are striving for, the wedding ring, is seemingly unattainable. In general, when Black women become mothers and are raising their babies, the attention placed on all of the above is no longer their focus, to the same degree. Some Black mothers focus on survival, if resources are limited. Others focus on achievement as they see the innate capabilities of their children and they strive to give them all that life has to offer and reduce any potential for them to suffer, financially or otherwise.

Most importantly, like any other mother, Black women love their children with all of their hearts and souls. The love comes from the core of their being, as their bodies release these children from within them. Their hearts are opened and the strongest of Black women become vulnerable and simultaneously warriors for their children. They become their Teachers, (before and after school). They are their caretakers, their cheerleaders and they carry this into their adulthood. When those children reach young adulthood, this society then tells those Black children to separate from their parents and leave the nest as soon as soon as possible, branding them weak and leeches off of their parents, if they do not leave. In some cultures, this is not the case as the children stay with their parents until they marry and will take care of their parents when they are elderly, bringing them into their homes. The departure, in American society, of adult children from parents, is applauded as independence and embraced as a successful accomplishment. Any adult child that does not "launch" is considered weak, incompetent and is accused of getting over on their parents, even if they work and contribute to the family household. The Black mother is generally not honored in this process. Black women often give away all of their love to their children and are expected to do so. By the time they are older, they take pride in their children's accomplishments, if all goes well, and the mothers are usually exhausted and grow weak as time progresses. When/If there is a crisis, they will muster up the strength and handle their grandchildren and help in any way they can. If only Black adult children could see their parents' (at this moment, I am focusing on mothers) sacrifices for them, throughout the duration of their lives, perhaps they would stand up and give her a standing ovation and more. Black Love begins with Black motherhood.

Exercise III

Black Parenting

If you are a Black mother or father, think about your parenting approaches and explore whether it is rooted in Black love. Go back to the first Exercise above and pick five words that resonate with you from the list. If you are fostering those words in the life of your child(ren), no matter how old they are, applaud yourself. My five chosen words from my Exercise One list are:

BLACK LOVE IS THE ANSWER

Strength

Generosity

Intelligence

Humor

Authenticity

Again, do not select any negative words from your list. Try to eliminate all negativity from your mind as you go through this process. Then, explore your five words in depth. Below are examples based on my chosen words:

Strength—As parents, my husband and I always pushed our children to be strong, by believing in themselves and to go for what they want in life. Everything, we taught them, was usable for their good, even when we were feeling weak, because it was merely an opportunity to rise up.

Generosity—We were generous to our children, to a fault, always giving them what they desired, perhaps, too much. If it was within our means and they wanted something, we tried to acquire it for them. We never let them struggle, which was perhaps to their detriment, but we are unapologetic about ensuring at all times, that their needs were met.

Intelligence—We nurtured our children's intelligence, ensuring that they were educated to the maximum. When they were little, beyond school, we read to them, took them to the library, traveled internationally, extensively with them, answered their questions with thoughtful responses, exposed them to art and music, and ensured that they were familiar with and had access to technology, as it emerged. We ensured that they understood Black history by reading to them, showing them films, nurturing them in Black spaces (Dance Theater of Harlem for our daughter, A Black-owned karate school in Harlem for our son, etc.). We nurtured their minds, bodies and spirits, knowing that all of this would lead to enhancing their innate intelligence.

Humor—We laughed with them a lot. Children love to laugh and are down-right silly at times. Nothing made us happier than to see them smile and giggle. We watched funny movies, went to amusement parks, vacationed at the beach and more. We ensured that they had games to play and extracurricular activities where they could socialize with other children and express their creativity. I was their pre-school Teacher at home to make sure that they had art stations, were read to, spent ample time outside and took swimming lessons, as an example. Our daughter, who loved books, was reading at 3.5 years of age, as I taught her to do so, before she went to Kindergarten. We enrolled them in summer camp, every summer, where laughter and fun was the focus. We let them visit friends and their friends visit them, welcoming them all into our home and we made sure that they both learned how to drive. All of this fell under, what we believed was humor/fun which was very important to their growth and development

Authenticity—We let our children see us, to a certain degree. There was lots of joy as they grew up, so we showered them with that, but limited a lot of the pain. For example, funerals, sickness in the family and etc. were shared with them with kid gloves. The authenticity really represented itself in terms of how we carried each other with others including the straightforwardness of our demeanor, our physical appearances (e.g. my natural hair) and our handling of their school matters with power whenever anyone got out of line in dealing with them. We exhibited to them spiritual strength rather than religiosity (although they were both baptized in the church and spent additional time in churches with us) and the fact that we love being Black. We showed our children

BLACK LOVE IS THE ANSWER

our Blackness as a real, authentic attribute of who we are, with great pride.

Once you have fleshed out your list, reflect and embrace yourself. Do not worry if you did not/are not achieving perfection as a parent. Just know that with your Black children, where you have to go that extra yard in this society, you did/are doing the best that you can based on what you knew/know at the time and that guilt, for anything that you think you are not achieving/did not achieve as parents is a useless, wasteful emotion. Guilt represents the past, not the present. The past is gone. It no longer exists, except as memories. The future is not here yet, so all we have is the present. Revel in the present, because tomorrow is not promised to you.

Everything that has happened/is happening with your children is part of your spiritual growth as well as theirs. Black family love is Agape Love. It is unconditional. As Black parents, Black love is not for the benefit of ourselves but for our children, a tribute to our ancestors and future generations. Always keep in mind that as Maya

Angelou so eloquently said, "Do the best you can until you know better. Then, when you know better, do better."

Eight

♥

Baby Makes Three + One

Young Black men often do not get their due in terms
of positive depictions of them in American society.
There is not a clear understanding, in the media, films,
and other mediums, of young Black men regarding how
they love their wives and children, how they are impacted
by their families and society, and the outcome of
positivity that is often generated from their cumulative
experiences, rather than the negativity that is shown to
the masses. I conducted this interview with a young man
who was one of my former university students and now
he is a husband, a father and a professional basketball
player. I knew him as a student to be polite, respectful,
diligent about his school work and his commitment to the
game of basketball. Now he is definitely someone who,
through his words, enlightens us about what it means to
him to be a Black husband and father in this nation and
what that experience is like on a day-to-day basis. I hope

you enjoy our dialogue, but more importantly, I hope you pick up on the positivity he exudes as he explains his involvement and insight about his various roles. Hopefully, he will be viewed as a positive example in an effort to counteract all that is exhibited in the media about Black men, as husbands and fathers, which is often overwhelmingly negative.

DeQuan Jones

DeQuan Jones is a professional basketball player who began his career with the Orlando Magic in 2012. He currently plays for the Nishinomiya Storks and resides in Japan with his wife, Allison, and daughter, Harper. While the Atlanta area will always be his home base, professional basketball has taken him to many places in the world. DeQuan has played in Japan, France, China, Italy, and Israel. Before DeQuan began his professional career, he graduated from the University of Miami, where he majored in liberal arts and political science. DeQuan has a deep-rooted passion for philanthropy and an undeniable love for working with young people. He prides himself on being an agent of change and hopes to combine his passions for basketball, being an advocate for youths and to break into coaching post-retirement.

DeQuan, Allison and Harper Jones

Rose Truheart: How did you and your wife meet?

DeQuan: She is going to deny it but she reached out to me initially, but it was all in good faith. We met through my ex and whenever I tell the story I always say, my now wife, Allison, was classy. Allison reached out and I was like, Hey, I am going to the University of Miami. I am pretty excited. What about you? But, the first time we actually met was at the Coca Cola Send Off. Everybody leans back in their chair when I tell this story. So, I was dating a young woman and my high school is known for producing top-tier athletes. So, this young lady, my ex...we had mutual friends. We started dating, whatever, and I noticed that she was a little more advanced than me, meaning her family was already kind of breeding her to be a basketball wife, like at 16. I would be away for basketball and she would call my mom and say: "Hey, you know, I just wanted to stop by and clean DJ's room because I know you mentioned that his room was not tidy. I just want his room to be clean." My mom was like, "Yeah, no, we are not doing that." So, we had this high school drama relationship. Her parents would get involved and they would call me and say "Just take her back. Give her another chance. She will be better." It was way too much for me at the time. I was uncomfortable. So, I said "we can be friends." About a month later, she said "I have a friend who's going to the University of Miami. You all could get to know each other." And she kind of connected us and Allison reached out to me. We exchanged numbers and talked, kind of like friends that whole summer. So, one of the executives at Coca Cola was a University of Miami alumni. His gift, I guess, for, the Atlanta graduates was to throw a Coca Cola Send Off Party at the World of Coca Cola, headquartered in downtown Atlanta. So, if you lived in Georgia, and you got accepted to the University of Miami, and you were enrolled in the upcoming Fall, you could come to the party. They had food, beverages and you kind of got to know, your classmates, mixing and mingling. A lot of the Miami alumni would come and speak and kind of talk about their experience at UM, in a great environment. It was cool. That was the first time I actually met Allison in person.

Rose Trueheart: I see.

DeQuan: I remember, her walking in late, as she does, and she took my breath away. I was like who is that chocolate beautiful girl? Who is this? I remember sitting down thinking, well, I am a cool guy and this is the first time I am tripping over my words. I was sweating in my armpits. I remember, that she was talking and it was like a movie. She was talking and I was seeing her mouth move but it was like the movie was on mute and I remember thinking, this might be my wife. From then on, we have been inseparable.

Rose Trueheart: Wow, you knew right away. That is beautiful. Did you consciously choose to marry a Black woman? And if so why?

DeQuan: Absolutely. I think my decision was rooted in, I hate to say it, but childhood trauma. I am probably the darkest of my cousins growing up. I was born in a small town in rural Alabama, Livingston, Alabama. I am fortunate enough, even now, to have my great grandmother in my life. My great grandmother is 97 years old.

Rose Trueheart: Well that is fantastic.

DeQuan: She is still of sound body, mind and spirit. I can still call her and we can have a conversation. She remembers who I am. But, I mention that to say that on my mother's side, my great grandmother was alive in the early stages of my life. And her being a fair skinned woman and growing up in rural Alabama, you can imagine the things that she experienced and the things that she went through. Naturally, I was treated differently than some of my siblings who were of fairer skin. I think that actually caused a rift between my mother and her grandmother, just name calling, but again, hindsight, and maturity teaches me that she was a product of her environment. So, I was raised, even at a young age, with pride in who I was. I was forced at a young age to look inward and find that beauty and kind of fight the outside world for what I was perceived to be. I knew that growing up, I would not find or foster a love that I wanted unless it was with a Black woman. Black women understand our plight as Black men, maneuvering in and operating through the world. I just wanted to repopulate the world with beautiful brown babies and teach them knowledge of self and self-love. It was a conscious decision.

Rose Trueheart: It is interesting how our lives shape who we become, particularly, the experiences that we have. They do not happen by chance. You have been married for quite a considerable period of time. It is longevity. Eight years married and together for 13 years is quite some time. What do you attribute to the longevity of your being together? Why do you think it is working and sticking?

DeQuan: I think the foundation of our marriage is friendship. We find in each other a great friendship. It is a great camaraderie. I think the foundation of us being friends is what makes the foundation strong. I give a lot of relationship advice to my single friends and I always tell them that, from the outside looking in, it seems as if people put up a front or a facade for what the other person wants or needs, in order to get access to that person, as opposed to being unapologetically yourself. In a relationship, and then a marriage if that foundation is not solid, when you meet adversity as a couple or as individuals, that facade comes down, and it is like, oh, man, this is not who I married. This is not who I chose to spend the rest of my life with. I think, for us, it is our foundation of friendship and our ability to be unapologetically who we are, who God made us to be. I was actually talking with a friend about the flower gardener concept of love. Everyone always thinks that, or has a partner, that they think would be perfect if she knew how to cook or if she was a painter, etc. But, the idea is that God already made them who they are supposed to be. If you have a flower, you do not try to change a sunflower into your concept of what you think it should be. As a gardener, you nurture that, you water that and you provide that with the space and the energy that it needs to blossom and be their full self. I think that has always been the foundation of our marriage and our relationship. ,

Rose Trueheart: I definitely understand that. That is fantastic. I love the way you put that. That was just lovely. I know you have a little girl, but I am going to ask you this question. How many children do you have, just for accuracy? And her/their names?

DeQuan: Just one. Harper Gwendolyn Jones. She is the light of our lives with so much personality. She is energetic!

A RETURN TO BLACK LOVE

Rose Trueheart: She is beautiful. I have seen pictures of her and oh my goodness, everything about her is sweet. She is just adorable and your wife dresses her beautifully. I guess you are part of that too. Let's not assume, but he is adorable.

DeQuan: Thank you. I am just the sponsor. My wife has the fashion direction and everything else. I am just there for fun.

Rose Trueheart: You both should be so happy. Oh, my goodness. How thrilling. And how old is she?

DeQuan: She is 18 months.

Rose Trueheart: I know what that means. She is hitting two. Get ready.

DeQuan: I mean, it is funny. We received the greatest compliment that I think we could have received as parents, when speaking with my father. We had a teammate over. We were getting to know each other. My teammate, looks over at Harper and he goes, "Man, I am going to be honest, bro. I have never seen a happier baby than Harper. I have never seen her cry. She is always happy." I think as parents, we fixate on what people say like "Oh, you know, they have to drink three glasses of milk every two hours or "They have to weigh 20 pounds at this age." But, in speaking with my mentors or my father, they are like, as long as your baby is happy and healthy, that is all that matters.

Rose Trueheart: Yes, I would agree with that 100%. The most important thing is joy for them and not all the rules. Those come later. Let babies enjoy and figure out who they are. As a Black father, do you think that there are any unique aspects in your approach to parenting Harper? Have you been actively involved in her life? And if so, how? Just give me a couple of examples.

DeQuan: I think the difference is perception. I think for Black fathers, the standard is demonization. Because of mainstream media and the perception the general public has about "absent Black fathers" is almost as if Black fathers overcompensate to kind of counter attack that perception. I think that is the biggest difference.

Rose Trueheart: So, you think that maybe you are saying that Black fathers may do more for their children than other fathers? Is that what you are saying?

A RETURN TO BLACK LOVE

DeQuan: Yes. Ma'am. Yes, they might try to.

Rose Trueheart: Again, why is that? Why do you think that would be the case? Please clarify your point a bit more.

DeQuan: I think that with the plight of Black men, historically, the absent father, that we have grown to experience, whether that be due to drugs being infiltrated into inner cities, the 1994 crime bill, was just pure negligence. It is like, we grow up spiritually, trying to overcompensate for the failures, or the perceived failures of our fathers. I think, from a spiritual standpoint, it is like, we have to do more. We, I think, experienced greater pressures, because we are trying to, in some ways, break those generational curses. We are trying to overcompensate.

Rose Trueheart: Have you been actively involved in in your daughter's life? And if so, how? For example, do you change diapers and do feedings and all those kinds of things? How are you involved?

DeQuan: Yes, I do diapers. I do feedings. When Harper was born, we kind of had a system. I am more of a night owl so anything from 10pm to 5am, was kind of my jurisdiction. Also, I just enjoy spending time with her. Even back home, we were going on walks or just taking her out for a stroll. Or even if I just took her outside in our garden and kind of talked to her, because I feel like, personally, those are spiritual deposits. Whether she grows up with any recollection of that, I feel like those connections cannot be duplicated. I think a lot of people, a lot of fathers, neglect that and think that she is too young to remember this or she will not even have any recollection of this when she gets older. But for me, it is more so like a spiritual aspect. Yesterday, for example, I know my wife being here by herself, gets naturally tired. She needs some alone time. She needs time to feel and do for herself. So, I had an early day. I was done with practice and everything at around noon and I just told her, sweetheart, just go and do what you want to do. She went and got a massage and it was supposed to be her day, but she ended up shopping for Harper. I guess that is a mom thing.

Rose Trueheart: Of course, I get that.

DeQuan: Right. And so, you know, what? When her mom came back, it was still like a spiritual connection to me. I can tell the difference when I have spent all day with her, versus when I am just in passing, like going to work. I am sorry. That was a long answer.

Rose Trueheart: No, no, that is fantastic! I really appreciate you sharing in that way because what I am trying to understand is the role that Black fathers play because there was a CDC study recently that says that Black fathers are, in fact, very active in their children's lives. And what I am trying to get at is how, in what ways and so forth. This can be shared not just as research, but really coming from the hearts of fathers who are doing it. I really appreciate your sharing with me that way. I am going to transition to another type of question, but it is very important, and that is, as a Black father, do you think that history, lineage and legacy are important in terms of your family, and if so, how?

DeQuan: Absolutely. I think as a parent and as a Black father is important to realize that your children did not ask to be here. I think that it is important because, for instance, I look at what my father, or my parents did for me, as far as history and, like you said, lineage. I think it is important for us to understand that we are the last defense for our children and that we must instill not just the idea of where we are going towards in the future, but also our lineage. For me, I always found security and safety in my lineage, meaning my great grandfather was an accomplished Veteran. He served in the Vietnam War. He came home and became a Firefighter and he retired as a Firefighter and a Farmer. I remember as a child, looking up in my great grandmother's house and seeing this big photograph of him in his Navy uniform and I remember thinking, wow, I want to be as accomplished and as respected as he is and was. My dad always instilled in me that we are a family of fighters. We do not give up, we endure, and we persevere and I think all of that goes hand in hand with a central theme of our lineage and that is something that we want to instill. That is something I have always found peace in when I met adversity in my life. So, I think that lineage and history are extremely important, because that is what held me personally throughout my life.

Rose Trueheart: Excellent. What about legacy? Do you think it is important for Black people to think about what is left behind for their children and for their family?

DeQuan: Absolutely. I think especially if we look at how Black people are disenfranchised. We have to consider the socio-economic gap. I think that is the most important. When you are socio-economically oppressed, you leave yourself open to harm, whether that is on the educational front, health-wise, living in food deserts or not having access to clean natural foods. So, I think that is very important and I think that we are seeing from our personal experience, a shift in Black people, especially being more financially in-depth. For me, especially, when I found out that I was going to be a father, I always had health insurance, but that was at the forefront, and getting life insurance, in the event of my untimely demise. I realized and according to research, that a lot of multi-generational wealth was built off of one insurance policy. I think that is probably the most important legacy to leave behind. To make sure that your kids are economically compensated is important because again, that is what I always lean back on. Our kids did not ask to be here.

Rose Trueheart: In regards to what you mentioned before, about what you say to other Black men, what message would you offer to young Black men who are dating and thinking of marriage at some point in the near or distant future, particularly in terms of Black women? What kind of advice would you give them?

DeQuan: My advice would be, what do you want your legacy to be? I look at my wife, as a shining example of what I have always dreamed of. When I think back as a kid, and I thought about what my wife would be, she embodies every quality of that. I always considered when you get married, the goal in most cases is to procreate. Would you want to procreate and make an exact carbon copy of this person to contribute to the world and to society? And if the answer is no, then you know, it is up to you, but I think that is my advice. That is the basis that I have always operated under.

A RETURN TO BLACK LOVE

Rose Trueheart: Wonderful. What are the most important aspects of marriage, from your vantage point? What do you think really stands out?

DeQuan: The most important aspects of marriage is intimacy and not intimacy just in the physical form, but also the intimacy of vulnerability. expressing your fears and insecurities and helping one another navigate this maze, that is the world. I think that is the biggest advantage you can have. As men we are not that spiritually in depth as we would like to think. Women have been blessed with the gift of intuition. Whereas men, we mostly operate off of ego and brute strength. I view my wife's intuition as an asset, as something that has helped me navigate the world and kind of see things and not really crash into a wall unnecessarily. Also, she has leaned on me for strength and protection. So, I think it is just operating on what each other can offer spiritually, emotionally, and the intimacy of being vulnerable and just partnership, and companionship. I tell people all the time It is not me versus you versus the problem. It is always us versus the problem. It is always us versus the adversity.

BABY MAKES THREE + ONE

Rose Trueheart: Excellent. We have just one more question after this one. Do you think, in terms of Black men as husbands and fathers, that their educational level matters relative to the educational status of the Black woman that he marries?

DeQuan: I personally think that is subjective and, in some instances, especially by mainstream media. That has been a tool to drive a wedge between the Black man and the Black woman, to an extent. I was in a restaurant, and I overheard a woman having a conversation with another young woman. She was thinking about marriage, getting engaged, and the one thing that the woman said that bothered her was that she does not believe that the man can be a spiritual leader, for their household or their family. And so, yeah, that got me to thinking. I think with marriage and Black men, especially, we hold a certain degree of intellect and a certain degree of knowledge that may not be documented on paper. But, I do think that based off of life experiences, we definitely qualify more than others, in most cases, to be the head of a household. I think that it is a tough one.

A RETURN TO BLACK LOVE

Rose Trueheart: Yes, it is a tough question. I do not know why, but I have noticed in the interviews for this book that this question, for whatever reason, is a challenging one. It is probably one that most of us do not really think about, because it is a societal thing more than who we really are. But, at the same time, it is necessary for our survival in this society. It becomes a struggle to answer the question and that is why I am asking it because it is something I really am trying to get at. Does this matter to us as Black people or not? And if so, or if not, how do we think about it?

DeQuan: I think it matters but I think there has to be, I guess, some level of compromise as it pertains to our survival, and our advancement as a race. I think that so often, even from our perspective, like, combatting white supremacy, combatting systemic racism, I think it all goes back and it has come full circle. The only way to break the mold and to combat those things are Black love, restructuring, or reinforcing the Black family structure. Two parent homes and the love and the confidence that constructive and positive Black family structures provide to kids growing up, is important.

Rose Trueheart: In terms of your household, educationally, you and your wife are both college grads, right?

DeQuan: Yes. My wife has a Master's in Marriage and Family Therapy.

Rose Trueheart: Oh, really? How wonderful.

DeQuan: She does not practice, but, she has a Master's and she has completed, I think 30 plus hours of interning. I do not know how that works, but she has had a year working with a private practice and she shadowed.

Rose Trueheart: So, she interned?

DeQuan: Yes. Well, she could get her certification at any moment. I cannot even remember how. She broke it down to me, but yes, she does have a Master's in Marriage and Family Therapy.

Rose Trueheart: So higher education for the two of you, is something that is in place because in some cases, one person received higher education and the other did not, and so forth. So that is part of what I am exploring.

A RETURN TO BLACK LOVE

We are at the last question. It has two parts. Do you have any parting thoughts about Black love and Black parenting? Do you have any pearls of wisdom that you want to share here before we end?

DeQuan: Yes. I think Black love is one of the foundations for dismantling systemic racism, systemic white supremacy, and for reinforcing our place as Black people on this planet. I think that the trajectory of our success is dependent on how much we pour into each other, how much love, and how much attention and affection we pour into our counterparts. I think that Black love is everything.

Rose Trueheart: I love that. Black love is everything. Well, that was a fantastic interview. I really want to thank you for sharing so much detail.

Nine

Sankofa: Return and Get It

Sankofa is an Adinkra term, from the Akan tribe in Ghana, which essentially means, go back and get, or more literally, "it is not taboo to go back and get what has been left behind." During the past two years, families have experienced all kinds of upheaval and mishaps, trying to stay together, in the midst of an insurmountable crisis, that has so many tentacles, that it is hard to understand. But, as Black families, we must get whatever has been left behind, no matter the circumstances, and bring it back as we have gained a great deal of knowledge and insight about who we truly are and what matters to us. What has been deemed a global health crisis started just at the tail end of the Year of Return, 2019, shortly after I returned with my family from a memorable trip to Ghana, to explore our roots.

That journey solidified my belief that what must be front and center, for Black families, is Black Love. There is a term that resonates, bearing the need for such Black solidarity in mind, which is Agape Love. Agape love, refers to unconditional love. It is lofty, moral and in my view, sanctified. When I think of Agape love, I envision my husband and my two, adult children. This love is unconditional as it is based on my being with people in a way that was created by a power greater than ourselves. We must not relinquish it, now or ever. We must hold onto it for dear life and recognize its value. It is precious and it is real.

There are some tenets that are essential to the Black family within the context of Agape love. Young Black people must first and foremost, respect and honor their parents. This begins with parents as they must teach their children how to speak to, value, and appreciate them. Children, as they are growing up, must be disciplined. I do not mean physical discipline, but rules and requirements must be set and the children must learn to follow them. As the children grow older, after being nourished, cherished, and loved by their parents, the young adults must offer their parents great respect and recognize that time is not unlimited. Sometimes, children are abandoned or mistreated by their parents, but that is another discussion, as here I am referring to scenarios where the parents have loved, cared for, and sacrificed for their children. Most parents put the needs of their children first. Many give them any and everything that they want, enabling a life for them with minimal trouble or despair. Grandchildren may arrive and all have the opportunity to participate in enjoying the new, young Black children in the family, with the same love and nurturing and with the wisdom of the grandparents at hand.

Consequently, if all goes in the order that it should, the children will outlive their parents and will ensure that their parents are taken care of until their demise. Those are full circle moments, from cradle to grave. This approach to Black Love ensures that the next generation will come forward with history and legacy in mind, enabling stories of love, abundance, care and nurturing in the present and future.

Understanding and Valuing Generational Differences

Black love is also understanding that the apple does not fall far from the tree but it can be intensely different from the tree. For example, father and son may look similar but not be "like father, like son" in terms of behavior. In order to be "like father" the son needs to be reared by the father, which may lead to similar behavioral characteristics, perhaps more so if the son is nurtured by the father. Otherwise, the son may adhere to his own nuances and ways, only, which will be his primary way of being. Behaviorally, the son may be more similar to his friends, a stepfather, or another person involved in his rearing. This is why care must be taken by the parents to be involved in the lives of Black children.

There is no doubt that we are living in a white, patriarchal society. I will not waste any time rehashing all that Black people have experienced trying to survive and thrive in this type of environment where we began, for the most part as slaves, helping to build this nation, without getting credit or monetary legacy for doing so.

SANKOFA: RETURN AND GET IT

Have Black people enjoyed the fruits of American society? The answer to that is a resounding yes, for some. However, one must also speak of the brutality, animosity, racism, disenfranchisement, aggression, mass incarceration, and the experience of feeling the impact of white "privilege," by many Black people. We are just supposed to negate that reality and only focus on what is good, although many Black people are still catching hell in this society.

Hence, I have decided that just as I refuse to use the term minority when describing Black people in this nation, where the demographics are rapidly changing to a point where Black and Brown people will be and are the majority in some locations, I also will no longer use the term white "privilege." As I see it, privilege has a positive connotation. It refers to a right. For example, if you are in a work environment and you meet or exceed a certain standard, you may be given the privilege of taking time off with pay. Privilege actually makes one proud. There is no way that anyone should be proud of unearned privilege. I cannot tell you how many times I have read or heard white people say something about how they benefit from white privilege and how they feel it is not right.

Many Black people constantly express concern about the privilege afforded to white people. But there is a problem with this kind of thinking on the part of all who discuss it. White skin is not an inherent privilege that anyone should honor above others. In fact, we should re-label the term white "hindrance." When people move through life benefitting simply by virtue of the color of their skin, whether they acknowledge it or not, it should be pointed out that this hinders others from achieving what they deserve/earn. Therefore, white privilege should be referred to as white hindrance. Hence, this kind of underserved benefit must be viewed as an impediment to the progress of others and must be stamped out wherever it is seen.

Specifically, the predominance of white people in academia, the arts, media, and every walk of life in the United States must end. We see Black people dominating in athletics as athletes, but those at the top, making all of

SANKOFA: RETURN AND GET IT

the decisions and earning the most substantial share of
the money, are largely white. All of this is white
hindrance because white people are taking most of the
premier spots and they are hindering Black people from
doing so. A concrete example is constantly displayed in
academia. Let's consider predominantly white colleges
and universities, which is the situation for most academic
institutions in the U.S. (excluding Historically Black
Colleges and Tribal Colleges) As a hypothetical example,
a President is hired at a college/university who professes
that her sole aim is to diversify, specifically, in terms of
Black faculty. However, the school defines diversity in a
very broad way, to include white women, other groups of
color, disability, etc. Now obviously, a broad definition
of diversity, on its face, is not a problem. But, what is a
problem is including these groups when the stated aim is
to hire additional Black faculty. The way this pans out is
that there is usually a search committee, which consists of
predominantly white people. The committee will accept
applications, which will go through a weeding out process
in Human Resources, based on algorithms or parameters

159

that are very rigid. When humans are involved, sometimes, Black people are weeded out, based on their names, which has been factually established as a process that occurs.

Subsequently, the Search Committee reviews the applications that are left, which in many cases after the aforementioned process has happened, leaves one or two Black candidates at most, if any. The Black candidates go through the process and the committee, utilizing the broad definition of diversity, takes an interest in the white candidates, who often times focus on Black issues as their core research and work, and who have published widely because he or she has benefitted from white hindrance. Afterwards, they choose white candidates and maybe one Black candidate to give a presentation as part of the selection process. Ultimately, these types of search committees often select the white individual(s) as the final candidates to present to the Dean. The Dean, who is most likely also white, concurs because she/he does not see the other candidates. The Dean selects from those candidates presented and sends that selection to the

SANKOFA: RETURN AND GET IT

Provost and President, who are most likely white. A white person is hired for the Faculty position and the Black people who applied have no idea what happened. The President then professes that the university wants to hire Black Faculty but cannot find any that meet their needs. Damn. If that is not white hindrance, what is?

Now the white woman who was hired, unbeknownst to her, has benefited from white hindrance and becomes the "diverse" candidate and the same process continues again and again. This is merely one example, in one field, but it resonates in different ways, in various predominantly white institutions/settings. Ultimately, this is not a privilege but a process, set up and designed to hinder Black people from achieving in an environment that is not set up to truly include them.

Many Black people, who do make it into predominantly white institutions, have worked very hard, have strived to achieve and have accomplished significantly. In academia, they may also find themselves subjected to a tenure process, where they have to go through yet another evaluation by people who perpetuate

161

white hindrance. The bottom line is that white people should not feel any comfort in what has been deemed white privilege, which is most likely viewed as an honor for them, but rather they should feel very uncomfortable about perpetuating hindrance for other people, which is wholly dishonorable.

The Desire to Return to Black Love

Some may say that I am one of the Queens of Diversity, Equity and Inclusion (DEI), since I have written books about it, given lectures, etc. But, I would say that the term DEI has run amok in the United States. There are people setting up and running DEI initiatives who have no idea what they are saying and doing, especially in terms of Black people. Again, going back and getting, it is Sankofa. Black people must retrieve that desire to love ourselves in our African, Black (Brown) bodies whether or not institutions want to diversify, promote equity and include us. Why do Black people constantly get relegated to a term or concept such as Black History month, DEI, Black Power and beyond. I

SANKOFA: RETURN AND GET IT

am not denigrating any of these terms and movements, because they have been extremely helpful to our advancement and challenging, and hence, must be applauded. But truly, is not it just about returning to loving ourselves as Black people? This includes that desire to want more that is Black including our spouses, children, grandchildren, son-in-law's and daughter-in-law's, Teachers, Educators, Models, Athletes, Professors, Doctors, Lawyers, brothers, sisters (I could go on forever), all in their glorious Blackness.

Black love includes a desire for Black children to have all of the opportunities available to them to accomplish whatever they desire and to live life to the fullest without hindrance due to the fact that they are Black. Black love is the ability to love one's self in all of our different hues, from light cream to jet Black and vice versa. It is the ability to love our hair, no matter if it is short, long, loosely curled or kinky; to love our noses whether they are wide or keen; to love our eyes, no matter their color, our shapes and body sizes from thin to thick, and to value and appreciate each other no matter our socioeconomic status, from poor to rich and everything in between. We are all connected by something that unifies us on an intrinsic level. We are descendants of the continent of Africa. We are Black. We are Africans living in the United States of America. Most of us are also Americans.

As we try to reconcile all that is necessary to experience Sankofa, we need to communicate with each other, effectively. To that end, I am closing out this book with Letters to different categories of who we are as Black people. My advice to you is that after reading these letters, of which you may disagree with some of my salient points, try to do the same. Whenever you have something to say that needs clearing out from your spirit, write a letter. Write a letter to any person you are having difficulty communicating with, whether they are physically on this earth in your midst or not, including your mother, your father, your children, your siblings, your friends, or whomever you need to reach out to. If you choose not to give the letter to them, that is okay, but at least the words will emerge and you will know that you wrote what needed to be written.

SANKOFA: RETURN AND GET IT

As Black people, we must begin the process of communicating completely, directly with each other, without other groups of people, as our frame of reference or at least releasing the words from our minds. The question is, what do we want to say to each other as Black people, to ensure that we see, hear and love each other, in all circumstances, at all times, when we need to, without reservation. With that in mind, I have written letters below. My letters are written in the context of my physical experience, as a Black, heterosexual woman, so use them as a mere guide, or as a jumping off point for who you are and what you want to say, because none of us can speak for everyone, nor should we try. Write from your heart, your voice, your mind and your spirit as I have done below. I hope my words, in my letters below, are felt from the sentiment in which they are given, which is Black Love.

A Letter to Black Mothers

Dear Black Mothers,

Generally, we rear our sons with more leniency than is the case for our daughters. Let us tell ourselves the truth

165

about this. Some of you may not do this and disagree. All I can say to you is respect. But, in an informal dialogue with some Black men, and as a mother of a Black man myself, I know that the most significant chores that some Black men have had to handle in their families, while growing up, was to take out the trash and maybe occasionally, wash the dishes. We cook, clean, wash their clothes and generally coddle our sons, because we love them. As an example, I had a very close friend growing up, whose actual name I will not use here but her nickname was Susie. She had six brothers, all older than her, except one. Both of her parents were busy, blue-collar workers. They worked long hours, so Susie's job was to cook, clean and take care of the house and her brothers, before and after school, since her mother was not around to do so. One day, I asked her why her nickname was Susie, which was so different from her actual name. She explained that it was short for "Susie Homemaker." I was shocked.

I used to visit her at her home, during our junior high school and high school years. Her brothers would call her asking for water, food and for her to bring them whatever they wanted, always yelling "Susie" to beckon her. She was responsible for doing the laundry, cleaning, cooking and making sure that when her mother returned home, there would not be much for her to do. Susie would accommodate every domestic request of her brothers and when her parents were at home, they would call her Susie, too. I remember sitting with her and her parents one day, as they praised me because I was college-bound. They said to me that they did not understand why she did not have aspirations. She does not even do her school work, one of them lamented. I was appalled. Out of respect for adults, I did not express my thoughts to them, but I understood why she never focused on herself. She was too busy taking care of her brothers and doing chores. I could not believe that they did not see that she was waiting on her brothers at all times, and had no time for herself, her schoolwork, etc. She got by at school and always passed every course but did not think beyond what was immediately in front of her. She wanted to marry and have children. Her brothers were completely coddled by her and her mother, when she was at home. Her father did not help around the house at all, but rather sat in his lounge chair calling her and her mother to bring him whatever he wanted. She did get married, but sadly, could never have children. I always wondered, because I never asked for personal details, if it was because of repressed emotions and that her body just needed to rest. She had done her mothering already.

Although this is an extreme example, it is not atypical, in terms of the coddling of Black men, as they are growing up, by mothers and sisters. I saw the same with my own brother. My husband was also coddled by his mother. I have reflected on this, trying to understand why this coddling happens with our Black sons. My conclusion is that perhaps the reason is because Black mothers are so worried about their sons and all that can happen to them, in the outside world, that we coddle them at home.

Whatever the reason, we must stop. We must get our sons ready to be a part of their families on every level. Black men must help Black women, with domestic responsibilities, so that they are not worn down and to make sure that our sons are raised to see themselves as part of the milieu of every aspect of the household, including all tasks, so that they will be fathers and husbands who will help their wives with everything as needed. The women who marry them are often the daughters that coddled their brothers, with their mothers. I was recently told about a Mother's Day meme that said Happy Mother's Day to all of the eldest daughters in the family. That speaks volumes.

In short, Black mothers, let's change this now. It will go a long way to help our Black men do better and be better in all aspects of their lives and to be prepared to be helpful husbands to Black women, in every aspect of the home, which we all want, because we love them so. It will also help our beautiful daughters receive them and have the support that they need to make it through, as they may one day become, or are already mothers. I love you Black mothers.

A RETURN TO BLACK LOVE

A Letter to Black Fathers

Dear Black Fathers,

   I guess the big question these days is what are you supposed to be doing as a father in this society? The answer is that nothing has changed, in that regard, from the beginning of time. You need to be present, to love the mother of your children and your children, as much as possible. Do not ever believe that your children do not need you. Your presence will enhance their lives because without you, although children will thrive, something will be missing. I know this to be true. As the daughter of a prominent Black surgeon, who was not present in my life, physically, for most of it, I missed something. I missed understanding the role of a father. I missed his hugs, my hand in his, his words, spoken directly to me, rather than through my mother, and an understanding of who he really was. His financial support was greatly appreciated but not merely enough to satisfy the quality time with him that I yearned for. I missed him grandfathering my children and will never know what that looks like, because he is now deceased.

SANKOFA: RETURN AND GET IT

I guess it all boils down to being there for your children, your family, however you can. Sometimes, doing so physically is not possible for myriad reasons, but your words to them, no matter how you can accomplish it, matter. Pictures of you, that they can always reflect on, also matter. When you are present, do for them. Hold their hands, lift them up, hug them, tell them that you love them, cook for them, eat with them, read to them, tell them stories of your life, and help them when they need you. Do not be afraid to say what needs to be said to your children, sometimes firmly, sometimes gently. If possible, travel with them. Let them see you treat their Black mother with love and care. Let them see you be strong and gentle. As a father, surely you are versatile. Let them know that.

The bottom-line is that your children absolutely need you, no matter the situation. If you must decide as to whether they need you or not, the answer is always yes. The financial aspect is also important. Be sure to provide for them, if at all possible. Give them whatever you have to offer so that they can see your generosity. We do not like to talk about that part, but it is real. Also know that money alone will never be enough. Essentially Black man, what is needed for every Black child, from their fathers, is Black love. We need you Black fathers. I love you Black fathers.

A Letter to Black Men (Who May or May Not Be Fathers)

Dear Black Men,

Let me begin by saying that we love you. When a Black baby is born to his Black mother, there is instant love and gratification. A beautiful boy. A Black Prince to love and cherish. We watch you grow from boy to man, changing in so many ways. Many of us do not know what to say or do, as perhaps we did not have fathers ourselves, who raised us. That was the case for me. I had no idea, the interaction between a boy and his father, because I did not see him with my brother. I merely watched my mother care for my brother. She was very gentle with him. Although her and I and my sisters would go at it, verbally, saying what we felt and thought to each other in gentle or harsh tones, we did not do the same with her son, our brother.

We still lost, that brilliant, handsome, young Black man, at the tender age of 31 so all of that protective care did not prolong his time with us. We loved him carefully. When you do become a man, Black men, we as Black women, beyond your mothers and sisters and other female relatives, are so excited. We want to meet you. We want to socialize with you. We want to be with you. We want to bring you home to our parents. We dream of marrying you; we want to have children and a family with you.

However, sometimes you do not see us. There are so many other women around, who are not Black. This society has told Black women, and you, that we are not beautiful and that white is right, thin is in and straight hair is better than kinky. It has told you that quiet is better than vociferous communication and that attitude is overwhelming. It has told you that big hips, thighs and breasts are just too much and that the food that we cook can be amazing but that is not enough. We know that.

A RETURN TO BLACK LOVE

You see, those are stereotypes. We come in all shapes, sizes and hues. We have brown skin, of various shades. It is not really Black. We know what you have been through and are going through, because we are going through it, too. We are very desirous of you and want you to be desirous of us, and only us.

We see you as ours. Somewhere, deep inside, we know, even if we live and move through the world in the United States, where most of us live as descendants of African slaves, that we are African. Many of us are also Americans. We may not say that or even know the facts historically, but when we look in the mirror, we see how we look. We see our hair. We see our curves and we know that all of this tells part of our story and who we really are. We do not want to be angry with you or have an attitude. We want to love you. This society has taken actions to make you scarce. There is mass incarceration, brutality, schools that do not cater to your needs, discrimination that slows down your achievement in society and beyond. These are all things that we know impact you harder than us, Black girls and women, in some ways.

We also know that you are beautiful. It is very exciting for us when you are accomplished in whatever you do. This society says get an education. Get your degrees and it will benefit you and help you to take care of your family so that the financial responsibility is not solely on us. But we know how tough that can be. For those of you who do achieve, whether it is academically, as Professors, Lawyers, Mechanics, Construction Workers, Plumbers, Doctors, Scientists, Architects, Musicians, Athletes etc. we think that it would be wise for us to build families together. With a Black woman, the two of you together, can build legacy, history and financial strength in the Black community, rather than giving all that you earned back to the white community that, often times, oppresses our people, systematically, rather than individually. Let achieving be your goal and then let's build together.

As a Black woman, I believe that we love and need you. Some Black women are alone, raising their children, struggling and trying to survive. But, with you, by our side, striving and working towards our betterment, we can do better as a people, together. I know this to be true. Until that happens, there will be so much pain between us. Some Black women will continue to whisper behind your back and give you vicious side eyes when you choose a woman other than us because we do not fully understand why, so we talk with each other, about you. I guess what I am asking brothers is, can we talk with you about this? How can we, together, go back and get each other? Let's talk about Sankofa. I love you my brothers.

A Letter to Black Women (Who May or May not be Mothers)

Dear Black Women,

Let me begin by saying you are loved. When a Black baby is born to her Black mother, the love exudes in the form of joy. A beautiful girl. A Black Princess to love and cherish. As Black women, we are not all mothers. For whatever reason, some Black women do not give birth. We need to have conversations with each other that does not solely revolve around motherhood. I must admit, that the bulk of my adult life has evolved around motherhood. Personally, being a mother has been the greatest joy of my life, in addition to being married to my husband. But, we are more than mothers. We think, we read, we work, we write, we cook, we dance, we love, we pray, we speak our minds, we care for ourselves and others, beyond children. We also study, achieve, run things, laugh, cry, exercise. In short, we do everything.

We need to be seen and heard. In that quest, sometimes, we get lost as this society does not fully see us. It often relegates us to basic accomplishments. It often objectifies us. It does not glorify us, but in some ways pities us. But you know what, that does not cut it, because as sisters, sometimes in our lonely silos, we hold each other up. I think of Maya Angelou, who was the first to tell us, that we are phenomenal women. I think of bell hooks who told Black girls that they can be happy to be nappy. I think of Gwendolyn Brooks who explained to us that there is a difference between aloneness and loneliness. I think of Alice Walker who explained womanism, as an option, for us, not just feminism. I think of Black women artists beyond writers (visual and musical), too many to name, who sing and draw about Black love, joy, and pain and what it feels like and how to make it through it all.

Many of us do something that helps us get through our lives as Black women. We cry. I laugh as I write this, because as Black women, we pride ourselves on being strong and not shedding tears at work, in front of our children, and in public spaces. We have been told that we have to be mega strong. But, as I get older, I find my salty tears to be healing waters. I have always heard the expression, "go to the water." I always thought it meant to go to the ocean, but I think that between the joy, laughter, the hard work, the caregiving, mothering or not, work and all the things that we do, we need to empty out. When we want to, we just need to cry until we cannot cry anymore, when and where we want to, and feel the vulnerability rather than strength, at all times and watch how people react to it. Do they reach out and hug you?

SANKOFA: RETURN AND GET IT

Do they walk away? Do they bring you a tissue, wipe away your tears and talk you through your pain?

Black women, you are so strong, beautiful and powerful. Perhaps it is time for us to release all that we have been carrying. It is time for us to let go and have expectations to do for ourselves, to love ourselves and heal ourselves. My suggestion is to find a quiet space, at least once a day, alone, where you can listen to your own breath, perhaps light a candle, pray/write/read, gently exercise and most importantly, if needed, go to the water. Let the tears flow, when you need to and when they reach your lips let your tongue taste the salt because as my dear mother, who rarely let us see her cry until she was deathly ill would say, salt heals wounds. Be as vulnerable as you are strong. Black love is strong. I love you my sisters.

As you reflect on these letters, I hope you are inspired to write your own, within the context of Black love. If we can find a way to go deep within and look at ourselves as Black people, embracing all that we are, without apology to ourselves or anyone else for doing so, we can enjoy Black live in its fullness. No matter what happens in this society and the world at large, there is something that I have no doubt about. I love humanity in all of its beautiful diversity and within the context of that understanding, but first and foremost, I love being Black, unapologetically, which is the key to open the door to Black Love.

Ten

♥

NYC Newlyweds

Newlywed Black couples offer a particular kind of insight regarding Black love. Their perspective is fresh, nuanced and in the early phases of development. This interview is intriguing because it provides insight into how and why this couple decided to marry and what the driving force is for them to be optimistic about the future. They were delightful in their candor and were particularly open about many aspects of their union including of their participation in couple and individual therapy. When considering their words, optimism will arise as to what their future will look like, together, as a Black couple. Their love for each other penetrates all of what they have to say, as well as their understanding, from their collective perspective, that they are role models for other Black, young couples who may be considering long term commitment and marriage. Their open discussion about their love for each other is delightful, to say the least, but also provides an opportunity to learn about Black love based on their willingness to share very intimate aspects of their union together.

Maya Posey-Pierre and Marc Pierre

Maya is 30 years old. She is an Actress and Professional Development Trainer in education. She is a native of Birmingham, AL and currently lives in Brooklyn, NY with her husband Marc. Marc is 28 years old. He teaches high school literature for the NYC Department of Education. Marc was born and raised in Brooklyn, NY and is of Haitian descent.

NYC NEWLYWEDS

Maya Posey-Pierre and Marc Pierre

Rose Trueheart: How long have you been married and where did you meet?

Maya: We have been married for, oh my gosh, how long? I have to count it. We have been married for about eight months.

Rose Trueheart: So, you are actually newlyweds?

Maya: Yes, we are newlyweds.

A RETURN TO BLACK LOVE

Rose Trueheart: That is great. You are the second newlywed couple that I have interviewed. Can you tell me where you met?

Marc: We met in Brooklyn, New York, on the train platform.

Rose Trueheart: Oh, really?

Marc: Yeah. Maya was on her way to a date actually.

Maya: Is that part of the story always necessary?

Marc: I just saw her on the train platform. I approached her. Maya was wearing an AKA bag. She is part of a Black sorority. I wanted to show her that I know some things and that I went to college, too. I did not want her to assume that I was any guy off the street. I asked her an obvious question. I asked her "so you are an AKA?" She was like "well, duh." From there, the conversation started to flow. Eventually the train came and she asked me if I was going the same way so we began talking about work and school and stuff like that. When she was getting off the train, I asked her if I could text her some time. I said to her, "I think you are really beautiful" and I think she was surprised, right Maya?

NYC NEWLYWEDS

Maya: I was surprised. Not that he said I was beautiful but because we were not having a conversation about dating or anything of that sort. I just thought he was being a nice person. I did not think he was interested in me in that way. That caught me off guard.

Rose Trueheart: That is such a nice way to meet. Maya did you want to add anything else to that or did he sum it up completely?

Maya: I think he did a good job. He could have left the date part out, but he did a good job.

Rose Trueheart: Okay, so let's go on to the next question. Did you consciously choose to marry a Black person? And if so why? If not, why?

Maya: For me, yes, because I grew up in Alabama where as a dark-skinned Black woman, I experienced personally in the south, the paper bag thing; the whole paperback theory that if you are lighter than a paper bag, you have access to things that people who are darker do not have access to. Or you see that you have social status that darker people do not have and being a dark little girl, ironically, or maybe not ironically, I experienced mothers of little boys telling their sons that they wanted them to be interested in the light-skinned little girls. They wanted them to have pretty babies and by pretty babies they meant light-skinned babies. We were so young. I feel like we were not even old enough to be thinking about that. But, I can recall being in middle school and high school where moms are sort of like, you have to be with somebody lighter than you so that your babies come out lighter. And for me, once I started to get more affirmation, I guess about how dark skin was beautiful and being Black is beautiful, I always wanted to be a mother and it was important for me to marry a Black man. I had this dream of having and raising my Black children and also being in relationship with someone who understands my experience.

Rose Trueheart: That is beautiful. Marc, what is your thought on that question?

Marc: Yeah, for me, it is interesting, because we are a young couple. I am 28. Maya, turned 30. I have been with women who are not Black and I think that to me, there is nothing like coming home to a Black woman, or

Maya, per se, because there is a foundation or understanding of one's own Blackness or critical consciousness of who we are and what we represent. Because my last relationship was with an Ethiopian woman, I experienced lot of anti-Blackness. I dated this woman for two years and I met her mother. When her mother thought about a Black man, she had certain images that came up for her.

Rose Trueheart: I am sorry. That got a little muffled. What did you say? What type of woman did you date before?

Marc: Ethiopian.

Rose Trueheart: Okay, Ethiopian.

Marc: I experienced, maybe not from her directly, but from her family, a lot of anti-Blackness, from her mom specifically, and what she thought about the idea of Black men. For her, certain images came up that caused a fissure in my relationship with her daughter. I have been in a relationship before where we saw Black bodies being assaulted by police officers. I feel like I had to explain that to people. I think that was the case with women that

I have been with before, whereas with a Black woman, there is an understanding. I do not have to explain that. I think it is important for me to date a Black woman especially because the background is there. In the past, I feel like it got kind of confusing and wiry, if that makes sense.

Rose Trueheart: For clarification, the Ethiopian woman that you dated is an African woman, so she is a Black woman, correct?

Marc: Yes. 100%. But I think that there were some anti-Black sentiments when it came to American born Black people in this country because she was born in in Ethiopia. I am not sure if I am saying that clearly but yeah, that is what I have experienced, to some degree. I also think that being with a Black woman, there is the understanding of how we move in the world as people. I have a lot of anecdotes. I was dating a Jamaican woman one time, and I do not have anything against Jamaicans, but just in general. My experience, one time, was that, I forgot which person it was, but it was a police officer incident. She kind of invalidated what happened. I think that being with a Black woman there is an understanding. You know what I mean?

Rose Trueheart: You seem to be distinguishing between Black American women and Black women from other nations. I just want to clarify because this is interesting. With the person that you refer to who is Jamaican, was this a person born in Jamaica, or born in the United States? Does she consider herself a Jamaican American? There needs to be some clarity there. She was Black right?

Marc: Right. I think she was definitely American born. I am not saying that I specifically chose an American Black Southern woman to be honest about that.

Rose Trueheart: Did you consciously choose to marry a Black woman. Both of the women that you described, were actually Black. I do not want to confuse the reader. There needs to be a little bit of clarification here.

Marc: Definitely. They were Black.

Rose Trueheart: Ok. You have been married for a short time. What do you think will contribute to a lasting union? Whoever wants to go first is fine.

A RETURN TO BLACK LOVE

Maya: I will go first. We have been married for a short time, for eight months. We have known each other for almost five years. We were dating for four years before we got married. Throughout that process I think we still had some growing to do. But, we had a lot of experiences that make us great at communication. We went to therapy together and individually. We had to work through a lot of complications. But early on, I remember the difference between Marc being Haitian and me being southern. We worked through that. He did not understand what my family was saying. I did not understand what his family was saying. Our bringing those differences together was essential. We did it so fast. I think we just learned how to have the hard conversations within that first year of really being together, dating each other and things that we have seen. For example, our friends, other couples, who are not together anymore, we hear their stories while thinking that is so little, that is so small. But, I really think it is because we just learned how to have those conversations, how to listen to one another and respect each other's opinions, even if they are different. Before we got married, we had to become clear on accepting what was different about the other person. For example, there were religious beliefs that were different. Before we married we asked each other, are we okay with this? I feel like some people get married and they know some differences exist, but they do not talk about it. Then, when they are married it comes up. But we were very clear about what was a no and what was okay. I think as long as we do that moving forward, we are going to be okay. We are going to have a strong marriage. Also, one more thing to add to that. Family is important. That was one of the big things for us. We had to make sure. Some people can say, oh, you know what, I am not marrying your family. I am just marrying you. But for us, it was like no. We have to be okay with each other's family and have great relationships with family because essentially, to us, our marriage is the beginning of a new legacy. We did not want to be separate. We wanted to continue to build upon what was already there.

Rose Trueheart: That is wonderful. Marc, your thoughts?

A RETURN TO BLACK LOVE

Marc: I think that foundationally, faith is a big part for us. I think we went to couple's therapy, but it was through one of our Pastors that goes to our church. I think that helped a lot because I feel like it gave us the understanding that the relationship is not just her and I, but it is between her, me, and God. What that does to our arguments, or having discussions about certain things or difficulties, is that we come to a common understanding that it is not always about the way I want it or the way you want it but we want it together. We equals God, too. I think having a strong foundation that operates on faith really allows us to have good conversation. There are certain things that I will never say to Maya or do to Maya, because this commitment is between me, her, and God. If I do something to offend her, I am offending the God that I serve as well, so that also helps us out.

Rose Trueheart: That was beautiful. We are going to go on to the next question. What does quality time with each other mean to you?

Maya: For me it is uninterrupted time. There are so many distractions. Working from home during this pandemic does not help. Everything is on the computer and the phone is always in someone's hands. So quality time lately has been, can we put the devices away and can we put the outside world away? I think we have the best times with each other right before bed when there is no choice because, we still try to say let's not have the device in the bed. Or we will take a walk outside and just be with one another but to turn the outside world off works for me, for quality time.

Marc:. I think recently, I realized that quality time is just Maya and I away from the world because I am a Teacher. I am always working, working, working. I realize Maya and I are the closest when we are not working. Our vacation this week was amazing because it was just her and I. Usually, I feel I have the most fun when it is Maya, myself and other couples or other people in an activity, but it is her and I and that is okay. What that looks like is just sitting down eating together, watching TV together or just talking. What I have enjoyed the most between work meetings is a little hug, a kiss on the cheek or a rub on the back between those things, because it has been hard for us during this time.

Rose Trueheart: Both of you are Teachers, right?

Maya: I am not a Teacher. I am a Professional Development Trainer. I spend a lot of time training Teachers.

Marc: I am a high school English Teacher.

Maya: I am also an Actor.

Rose Trueheart: I did not realize that. Very interesting. You have the left and right brain going on here. I love that there is so much variety that we can find in our lives. We should pursue it because we have so much that we bring to the table. Let's go on to our next question. As a Black couple, do you think that there are any unique aspects to your marriage relative to other groups?

Maya: Absolutely. There is something about being multilingual. I think all Black people are, even if you do not literally speak another language outside of English. It is just the way we move through the world. We know, we have had to adapt to be comfortable in multiple spaces and we have done it so effortlessly with so much style and grace. When I walk into a room with Marc, or I post a picture with him, there is something about being a Black couple. It does not take anything away from anyone else's marriage, but it is just different. It is like living Black history. I think when people see us, and see other Black couples, they see the history and the legacy that we hold, as Black people. They see Kings and Queens and empires and future Black children. People who are going to continue to do amazing things, because Black people do amazing things. That is my take on it.

Marc: Yeah. I feel like it is unique because, growing up, what Maya and I have, I had never seen it before. I think that one of the obstacles that we faced in marriage, as I was telling my Therapist, was that I kept waiting for something like, some kind of TV relationship. I kept saying to myself, I am not ready to get married because I do not have what they have. And there are these couples I would look at on the TV screen. My mom and dad are not together. I do not know about people that actually are married. I realized the whole time that I was looking for something that I already had.

A RETURN TO BLACK LOVE

Once I realized that in one of my therapy sessions, I said, I am ready. I have been ready. Because for me, I am on the younger side. But, now I feel like Maya and I are models, because our friends are getting married now and I am like, welcome to the team. It is kind of cool because I think that it is unique, not only because I do not see it a lot, but now we get to establish a community of couples to talk to, relate to and do activities with because they all signed up for the love journey, Black Love. It is so great now, because Maya and I used to, a couple of years ago, just go to theme parties that had a lot of activities that were socially meant for single people. What Maya and I created was kind of a movement, where we host events for couples only and it has been so fruitful because it is a celebration of Black love where only Black love couples can get in now. That is the unique thing about it for me.

Rose Trueheart: That is great. I have been married to my husband, who is Black and I am Black, for 36 years.

Marc: Wow.

Rose Trueheart: Yeah. I am saying that to you both to let you know that it definitely works. My husband and I are best friends. Our story is in this book as well because we feel that we need to share how we met and other pertinent details.

Maya: Oh, that is so beautiful!

Rose Trueheart: Thank you. We have also traveled together, to over 50 countries.

Marc: Yeah? I have a question for you. I am curious.

Rose Trueheart: Sure. Go ahead.

Marc: Maya and I were traveling, and we saw another Black couple. We were so happy because they were young and they had kids. But you also have kids. Did you travel with your kids when they were young?

Rose Trueheart: Yes. Absolutely. Our children traveled mostly everywhere that we went, no matter where it was in the world, because we wanted them to have a global world view. We took them to Africa, Fiji, Europe and beyond. They have traveled since they were very young. In fact, some of our friends would ask us why we were taking the kids with us on our trips. They would ask if we ever want to travel alone. We said no because we need them to see what we are seeing. This is not to say that we did not have some time alone traveling, but we felt it was so important to broaden their worldview. My husband and I made sure that our children would see mostly everything that we saw and in fact, this did broaden their worldview. It was a joy to take the children with us. It was fun, because some of the travel was when they were really little. They only remember some of it vaguely now. But, some of it they do remember because we have been doing this for a long time. They are adults now. During the summer of 2019, we all went to Ghana together for the Year of Return. It does not stop. Of course, they travel on their own now because they are grown. But from time to time, we will say hey, do you want to go with us to wherever? Our daughter also went with us to Italy last summer. But when they were younger, we took them with us and I have no doubt that doing so was one of the most beautiful things that we did as a Black family. So, let's go on to our next question. Who is most actively involved in activities around the house, namely, the domestic activities like cooking, cleaning, and etc. and give me a couple of examples?

Maya: Oh. It is me. I am the most active doing all of the household things except for probably taking out the trash. We are laughing that you asked this question because Marc always comments, when we go to visit the South, about the gender roles. But ironically, that is what it looks like in our house. I do most of the cooking and most of the cleaning until I complain and then he does more of it. But I understand where it comes from. So yes, we are working on it. We are getting Marc more accustomed to cooking and cleaning.

Rose Trueheart: Marc, do you have a comment about that?

Marc: I mean, that is the way it is. It is a work in progress.

Rose Trueheart: As a Black couple, do you think that history, lineage and legacy are important in terms of your relationship and your future together?

Marc: Yeah, I want to get into that first. I feel like being with Maya, a Black woman, is important to me, especially, because for me, my family tree is not there. Except for my grandmother, I do not know anybody. And I think that for Maya and I, I feel like there is going to be an extensive, beautiful family tree. Our children will be educated and they will have done all sorts of things. I think that is so important. My grandmother's birthday is today. She is 90. I think it is so powerful. She called me today and said, I am happy for you and Maya and I want you guys to have grandkids. I feel so happy to have a grandmother that wants something from me. When we have children, we will be there for them and we can also provide for them. Their legacy gets to look very different because Maya and I both have more than what we were given. My mom scratched two pennies together and took care of me and my younger brother. I feel like I have my pennies now and I will be able to give my kids much more. So, I am so excited about our marriage, because I feel like our gift to the planet will be our seeds, our children. I cannot wait to be a father because I have so much more than what I was given. I cannot wait to see what it looks like. I guess in the continuation of a legacy that is written, captured, understood and documented, it is going to start here.

Rose Trueheart: Yes. Excellent. Maya, do you want to add to that?

Maya: The only thing that I would add to what Marc has already said about being a Black couple, and the importance of legacy and lineage is that people are seeing that now, with us being in a healthy marriage. It is so important that I think that is the whole reason that you are writing this book to document the positivity and the beauty and the love that Black marriages and Black couples have. We feel so fortunate that we have that. I think that before we have kids, people and our family are saying that wow, they are healthy. It is like being a unicorn. You are in this world. That is the whole reason we started bringing couples together, because we are like, we are here. The world is trying to tell you that we are not here, but we are here. My nieces and my nephews seeing me with Marc, I think they are surprised. My mom and everybody is surprised to see it. I am just excited that we are going to be together for a long time. We are going to continue to show the world.

A RETURN TO BLACK LOVE

Rose Trueheart: I think that is why I am writing this book. It is so important for us to share this because I think Black love is happening in our society, but we do not get to see it enough. We do not get to see stories told about it. We do not get to see many books written about it and we do not get to be put out there enough for the world to see us in a positive way. It is time for us to tell our stories. These success stories about our relationships are important, because family is part of our history and our lineage. It is not new to us as Black people. But, the society that we live in does not necessarily recognize it. It is upon us to make sure that our stories are told. I love what you both said. I think you are both very accurate. That is why I am conducting this lovely interview with you so people can enjoy learning about your love. You will not be, as Maya said, a unicorn. We are not unicorns; we are here. But, unless we speak and let people know, it is not going to be known. So that was fantastic. Let's go on to the next question. What message would you offer to young Black couples who are dating and thinking of marriage at some point in the near or distant future?

NYC NEWLYWEDS

Maya: I would offer that it is important to be whole spiritually, emotionally and mentally, before you decide to commit. Some people do not want to get married, and that is okay. But before you are in a serious, committed relationship, to be fulfilled, you should have all of those things together, because the trauma comes out. Until that trauma is dealt with, it can be difficult to be able to be in a committed relationship. You are no longer by yourself. I have seen, in a relationship, where there are two teams. It is no longer two teams anymore. They have to be one. I think that is a beautiful thing. But, if you are not ready to accept that, you might need to just play by yourself until you are ready for that. Coming home, and having to think about, what are WE going to eat, not what am I going to eat. How are WE going to get through a hard time not how am I going to get through it. It is constantly being able to open yourself up to thinking beyond just you.

Marc: Yeah. I always say the same thing. I think that I would ask the question, are you ready to stop being selfish? I am still learning that marriage is a call to be selfless. No longer do you think about your own self, but you think about somebody else. I would say that also do the self-work as well. I know that is what helped me arrive here was being in therapy, which has helped so much, because I was able to begin to iron out some of the things that show up in conversation. I think that having another place to pour out is a process. I get to also process those things outside of the relationship.

When we were first dating we had so many people ask us if we were moving too fast? It is true.

We realized that they are scared. They were projecting their fear onto us. And here we are almost five years later, and thank God we are still together. We are happy. We are healthy.

Rose Trueheart: You are both speaking so beautifully about your marriage. And I think that is so important. There are a lot of things that you understand early on, which I think is just fantastic and will lead to a longer lasting relationship. What are the most important aspects of marriage from your vantage point? This is slightly different from the prior question around this.

NYC NEWLYWEDS

Maya: I have to say alignment is a perfect word because it hits multiple topics. I think that the important thing is that before we make decisions individually or together, we have to sit down and come together and make sure we both are okay with it. Usually, you are used to doing life for you. Now we are doing life with somebody else. You have to sit down and figure out how are we going to do this. We realized last year, that there were so many things that were going unsaid that we were not talking about. We had just been making assumptions until we said, wait a minute, where do you see us in five years? Having that conversation, we said, oh man, we are not in alignment. We could be doing two different things without even realizing it. So that is the most important thing.

Rose Trueheart: That is very good. Alignment is a good word here.

Marc: Yeah, I think I would say, its partnership. Two heads are better than one. I feel that there is a lot of things that I can do or get done. It is just a much better experience because I have a partner. My vacation this week was better because Maya was there.

A RETURN TO BLACK LOVE

Rose Trueheart: Where did you go on your vacation?

Marc: Costa Rica.

Rose Trueheart: Oh, how lovely. I love Costa Rica. It is such a naturally beautiful place.

Marc: Yeah. It was beautiful. It was so good. Everything we do is in partnership. There are a lot of things that we do together, whether it is going to do the laundry, the groceries and other domestic duties now. The things that we do together I find myself saying, this is good having a partner in this. There is an intimacy there that I cannot really explain. I have a relationship and having a partner for everything, when it comes to big decisions, is great. Maya's strengths are a lot of my weaknesses. I am not good with time. Maya is really good with time. Maya is not really good at always saying what she wants outside of the relationship. I will say, do not worry, I do not care. I think there is a harmony that happens in our partnership that I think that is the best thing. It is the completion.

Rose Trueheart: So, you complement each other?

Marc: Yeah, exactly.

NYC NEWLYWEDS

Rose Trueheart: Great! On to our next question. Do you think that educational level matters relative to each other? Should couples that plan to marry consider this?

Maya: That is a tough one for me because I am big on experience. When we say education, are we just talking about academic education? Having degrees?

Rose Trueheart: Yes. Let me make sure the question is understood. The question is about higher education in an academic sense. The question is, do you think that educational level matters? When I say educational level, I mean, for example, if there is a couple in which one person did not get a college degree and the other did. Does it matter?

Maya: Marc may disagree with me here, but I am going to say no because as for me, I think I have seen some people who have gone to college, who have doctorates and in terms of a relationship, in terms of marriage or any committed relationship, they are still not great partners.

Marc: What about for us?

Maya: You having gone to college and gotten your master's degree definitely plays a role in our relationship,

207

because you have had experiences and higher education, that have allowed you to approach the world differently. You were way more mature when I met you because of your educational experience, because you had to learn how to work with different people. But, I think that it is possible if I am not talking about us, and we are talking about just in general.

Rose Trueheart: Let's begin by exploring this in terms of the two of you. Then the second part of the question is should couples, in general, who plan to marry, consider educational level?

Marc: I think it is important. Yeah, it is definitely important, because most of our conversations that we have, are rigorous, to say the least, intellectually, and it helps that we both went to college.

Rose Trueheart: What is the educational parity between the two of you?

Marc: Maya went to the University of Alabama. She has a Bachelor's in, what is it again?

Maya: Criminal justice.

Marc: Because Maya was thinking of becoming a lawyer and she was also a big debater in high school. She has a lot of experience in debating. As for me, I stopped at a Master's at Columbia. It is a hard question to answer. I do not know if it really matters, but I think it factors into all of our conversations. When we have conversations, politically or anything, I feel like the angle that she takes is complex as a result of her education and critical thinking skills. I am a high school Teacher so I am thinking that someone who only has high school diploma, based on someone's educational level, you have some kind of critical thinking skills. I think that brings a level to the relationship that helps a lot whether it is about financing and planning, wanting to own a home or paying bills. That helps a lot. I guess I cannot speak too much in depth about it, though, because I feel like it is just a part of who we are.

Rose Trueheart: Now we are going to go outside of the two of you? I think you both answered that very thoroughly. Do you think that Black couples should consider this? Should they consider education in terms of planning to marry each other?

Marc: Although on paper I probably make more money than Maya, right? I do not make more than you Maya? No? Seriously. I guess I do not know what you make. I feel like for us, it does not really play like a dominating factor. The fact that I have more education than Maya, you probably would not even know. I think Maya's the smarter one to be honest with you.

Rose Trueheart: Getting back to you Marc, you went from this being about education to being about money. Therefore, let's talk about this in terms of outside of you. If you were talking to a group of young people, what would you say to them? Should couples who plan to marry and remember, again, we are speaking of Black couples, consider education as a factor in their union or not?

Maya: I am going to say yes.

Rose Trueheart: Can you explain?

Maya: Yes, because the level of education or higher education that someone has does have an effect on how they view the world and how much knowledge they have when it comes to approaching the rest of their life. Someone who has gone to college, oftentimes, has had to be in situations where they have had to do life on their own and figure things out. They have to figure out how to interact with different types of people. Typically, these people know about finances. There is more to higher education than just the academics that make you a well-rounded person. Also, you have to be realistic sometimes about the type of life that you want to live in the world that we live in. I would say this is not a hard and fast rule, but it does affect the type of opportunities that you have access to. The type of access that you may not even be able to, unfortunately, afford your children if that is something that you want to think about in the future. I am going to say yes.

Rose Trueheart: Marc, anything else? Or does your other response stand?

Marc: Yeah, I am still struggling.

Rose Trueheart: It is definitely a tough question.

A RETURN TO BLACK LOVE

Marc: Yeah, because I know, a lot of educated idiots too. I know a lot of people who did not go to school that have more than I do. I am still struggling with it. I am not exactly sure to be honest with you. But your question should be considered because, unfortunately, sometimes people approach and think of you differently, whether you went to school or not. Going for my Masters at an Ivy League did help me in some sort of fashion. I would say yes. I think it does. It does help.

Rose Trueheart: Alright. We are at our last question. It has two parts. Do you have any parting thoughts about Black love? Secondly, do you have any pearls of wisdom that you want to share?

Maya: These questions are not easy. I would say for people who are experiencing Black love, in terms of marriage or just committed relationships, it is such a gift. We are just so blessed. There is a level of understanding that we share because we are both Black. Not only that, but we get to showcase that to our future children, our family members, and to anybody who feels like that is not a thing. I do not have many words, just mostly feelings about Black love, which is just joy and happiness. It is what I think of swag. We just glow differently.

Marc: We look good too.

Rose Trueheart: Yes, these are words that you can feel. As a writer, I know that certain words also have feelings attached to them. I think those were excellently chosen words, which express what you are trying to say. Marc, do you want to add to that?

Marc: I feel like it is a celebration. I feel like we are on a 365-day holiday celebration all the time. I think that there are a lot of things going on in the world today in terms of just so much happening. I think the one thing that I am always happy about is my relationship. I always come back to it. I am happy that I have this Black woman in my life at the end of the day, ride or die. She will be here. I think my parting words are when the going gets tough, look for your wife.

Rose Trueheart: That is fantastic and that was a wonderful interview. I hope you enjoyed it as much as I did. The fact is that Black love always existed. We are not going to talk about it like it is a newfangled thing. It has always existed and we are just sharing stories of what we know is real.

Eleven

Longevity

Longevity, in terms of Black love and Black families is often left out of the stories told about Black people in the United States. The reality is that there are many Black families in which there are long, sustained marriages, where both parents are present and active participants in the lives of their children. It is important to emphasize that many Black women are enjoying intact relationships with their Black husbands, who are present and committed to the family. Black children are enjoying growing up with their fathers supporting them in every way. As a shining example of this, I interviewed Mr. Hubert Peterson (who I met as a friend in undergrad, where we all called him Hubie) depicted with his beautiful family below, to offer insight about his experiences as a Black husband and father in the United States.

A RETURN TO BLACK LOVE

Hubert (Hubie) Peterson Jr.

Hubert Peterson Jr., retired, is a graduate of Onondaga Community College and Lemoyne College where he earned an Associate Degree (A.S.) and Bachelor of Science Degree (B.S.) in Business Administration. He has served as a Commercial Insurance Underwriter for Nationwide Insurance Company and worked for other insurance companies as well as agencies/brokerage firms during a 29-year period throughout his career. Hubie enjoys a good round of golf, basketball, football, and tennis, as well as socializing with family and friends. He is also passionate about feeding the needy in the community with his home church, Jackson Memorial African Methodist Episcopal Zion (AMEZ) Church, located in Hempstead, New York.

LONGEVITY

Muriel Lynette Peterson, Traci Lynette Peterson, Hubert Peterson, Jr. and Patrice Diane Peterson

Rose Trueheart: I am very delighted that we are having this opportunity to discuss this particular topic. So, the first question that I have for you is how long have you been married?

Hubie: For 39 years now.

Rose Trueheart: You are about to hit 40 years. That is really wonderful. Where did you meet your wife?

Hubie: I actually met Traci when I was in high school. I have known her since I was 16 or 17, thereabouts. I was a junior in high school when we met.

A RETURN TO BLACK LOVE

Rose Trueheart: You are high school sweethearts. That is so beautiful. You have been together more than 39 years, which is actually the marriage but you have known each other a lot longer than 39 years, correct?

Hubie: Probably closer to 50 years, maybe?

Rose Trueheart: Did you consciously choose to marry a Black woman? If so or if not, why?

Hubie: I do not know that I consciously did it. I do not think I have ever dated any white girls so, I guess I did consciously do it.

Rose Trueheart: You had never dated a white girl before, but you had dated individuals other than your wife, prior to meeting her, correct?

Hubie: Yes, and after meeting her. We had a relationship that was interrupted, I think twice. We broke up. We went back together. We broke up again some years later. After that, we got married. There were two breakups.

Rose Trueheart: This was before you were married?

Hubie: One was in high school, and one was when we were adults

LONGEVITY

Rose Trueheart: You have been married for a long time. We established that. What do you attribute to the longevity of your union?

Hubie: I think the biggest factor in terms of our longevity has been, we actually love each other. We have grown together. I have learned things. I imagine she has learned things and we keep the lines of communication open. She listens when I speak, and I listen when she speaks. So, I think that is probably one of the key factors in in our marriage lasting so long.

Rose Trueheart: You mentioned that you have grown together. Being together for such a long time does give you an opportunity to grow together. How many children do you have?

Hubie: I have two daughters. They are a big reason that we are together also, because I could not see myself being separated from the two of them. I do not think Traci would want to be fighting me for custody of the kids. They are a big factor. She and I always say that we not only love our children, but we like them and that is beautiful. I have been blessed with two beautiful girls.

Rose Trueheart: That is so great and important. Traci is a dancer? Is that correct?

Hubie: Yes, She has done that, up until just this past year. She retired from teaching in the New York City School District. She was also teaching students at Hofstra and Hunter College. She just gave that up.

Rose Trueheart: She was teaching dance?

Hubie: Yes.

Dr. Patti Rose: Yes. I remember her being a beautiful dancer. Well, getting back to your lovely daughters. What are their ages?

Hubie: My youngest is 35 now. And my oldest is 38.

Rose Trueheart: They are adults.

Hubie: Yes, they are.

Rose Trueheart: What do you think in terms of your having adult children? How does that differ in terms of your being a Black father, to two daughters, who were, babies and then went through all of their phases, and now they are adults? How would you differentiate between them being children and adults in terms of your parenting?

LONGEVITY

Hubie: There is a significant difference between when they were children, and being adults now. When they were children, I loved them. I nurtured them. I listened to them. I included them and a lot of things, I shared with them. I am pretty much doing the same thing now and I provided for them. As adults, if they need something, I try and provide that also. It is really ongoing. It has pretty much been the same. Of course, they needed more attention. They needed more guidance when they were younger, but we have always had just a unique relationship. I will give you an example. I used to play a lot of basketball when I was younger and I used to go to a gym on Friday nights or Saturday mornings. The girls, when they were probably five or six years old, I would take them with me. They would get in the corner with their coloring books or their dolls or whatever they wanted to bring. I used to take them shopping with me. People used to think I was crazy for taking them shopping. But most of the time I took them to the stores where they wanted to go. They always have chairs and couches in malls. I would sit down and let them shop. We have always been close.

Rose Trueheart: That closeness is really important, which brings me to my next question. Again, this book is about Black love. I am focusing on that aspect of things. As a Black father, do you think that there are any unique aspects in your approach to parenting; anything that you would think is unique based on the fact that you are a Black man in the United States?

Hubie: I do not think anything that I did was unique, that I did for my daughters. I think all of the things that that I have done, or tried to do for my daughters, every father should do, when it comes to providing for and loving your children. You have to be all in for your children. Right? So, I do not think I did anything special. I may have done some things that other men have not done. But I do not think I have acted uniquely. But I did do their hair sometimes.

Rose Trueheart: Oh, really? You did their hair?

Hubie: Yeah.

LONGEVITY

Rose Trueheart: That is something definitely to talk about. I do not know if it is unique. But I do know that it is definitely special because that is quite challenging to do. As a man, it can be quite challenging to do a Black woman's hair, because there is a lot of sensitivity around Black hair, you know? So that is very interesting. I know you already gave the example of taking them with you for sports and shopping with them, and now doing their hair, but how long have you been actively involved in their lives? Were you involved with the taking care of their basic needs like diapering and feeding and all of those kinds of things and as their lives progressed?

Hubie: Let me just say this, I am the oldest of seven children. So, I learned how to change diapers. I learned how to wash clothes without putting bleach in the colored clothes. I did all of that for them. I cooked for them. I took my daughters anywhere they wanted to go. They were cheerleaders. When they were small kids, they were involved with Pop Warner, a Youth football and cheer and dance program. They were too young to drive so, I would always take them to that. As they got older when they went to the nail shop, if mom was not around, I would take them there, pick them up, get out the car and open the door because their nails were still wet. Those are a couple of things that I have been involved in. I took my oldest daughter to about five colleges that she was considering during her senior year. For my youngest one, I did not have to do as much driving around because she decided to go to Queens College right here in New York City. But the oldest, I took her to Clarkson University. I took her to where she wanted to go in state, and a couple of other colleges, in Pennsylvania. I cannot remember them all, but I took her to at least four colleges.

Rose Trueheart: Excellent. That is really great. So, you have been, overall, very active in their lives from the time they were born to their adulthood. Would that be accurate?

Hubie: That is absolutely correct.

Rose Trueheart: I hear college was mentioned so as a father to them, did you find education to be important? Did it have to be higher education?

LONGEVITY

Hubie: I expressed to them, as well as Traci, that when growing up, they had to be involved in some type of structured activity, and that they were both going to college.

Rose Trueheart: Okay, no question.

Hubie: No question.

Rose Trueheart: Okay, I hear that very strongly. I think that is very important to hear. As a Black father, do you think that history, lineage and legacy are important in terms of your family? And if so, how?

Hubie: I thought it was important for me to be the father that I have been and still am because that would give my daughters a sense of the qualities they should be looking for, in a future husband.

Rose Trueheart: We have a very unique history, as Black people in the United States of America. Our people largely came to the U.S. as slaves. There is lineage that is passed on. There are just a lot of things that we understand that are unique to us. Do you think that legacy is part of that when you are parenting? Is there anything that you tried to instill in your children based on that reality?

Hubie: Can we get back to that?

Rose Trueheart: Yes, we will come back to that. So just think about it. I know these questions are a little heavy, but these are the kinds of questions that help us to really dig in and understand what it means to be a Black father in the United States and to demystify some of the misnomers that are out there about how this takes place. The next question is, what message would you offer to young Black men who are dating and thinking of marriage at some point in the near or distant future? Particularly in terms of Black women? What kind of advice would you give?

Hubie: I would say, you have to definitely think about this. Take your time. Think personality--look beyond the aesthetic properties of a woman that you think you might need. You need to look for someone that perhaps likes some of the things that you like, and take a look at some of the things that she is interested in. And if there are things that you are not doing, do not shy away from them.

Rose Trueheart: Would you share one example, so I can be clear about what you are saying?

Hubie: A lot of guys are, I guess, connected with sports. So, for a guy like that, he might, if he is looking for, say a wife, then she has to like sports a little bit. Maybe not every sport that he likes, but she should at least like sports, not love sports, but like sports.

Rose Trueheart: I am laughing because my husband was an all-around athlete, including baseball, basketball, etc. in high school, and an athlete in college and now he is a Coach, in addition to teaching, after coming out of the financial world. He recently received the Hall of Fame Award from his High School for his athletic participation and I do not like sports that much at all. So, I find it really interesting that you say that because I think that over time, I have come to only slightly appreciate sports. And that is only some, not all sports, to be very honest. But, I will use golf as my example. My husband loves golf and so I wanted to know, what is this game that he loves so

much, that is something perhaps I can play? Then I
started trying golf myself. Now I enjoy it very much. I
think you have made a good point. Sometimes you
cannot see it right away. But, remaining open is a good
idea.

Hubie: I have another example for you. Traci does not
golf. She is not interested in golf. But I took her to a
couple of professional tournaments and she saw how
closely I was watching the players and I was having
conversations with people. So, she said to me, "You really
love this game, don't you?" I said, "Yes, I do." She said,
"Well you keep playing." It was a great demonstration of
support. Right? For me, and things that I like. She has
always been involved in dance and I have always
supported her. Most people think that I did not get any
exposure to dance until I met Traci, but I went to see
The New York City Ballet when I was 14 years old and
the Dance Theatre of Harlem because I was a part of a
program when I was a kid that developed appreciation for
the arts, so when I met her, I was like, Oh, yeah, I have

seen stuff like this before. I learned more. But, I did have some sort of foundation.

Rose Trueheart: Right. I guess what we are both describing here and correct me if I am wrong, is flexibility. Is that right? You may not be proficient in the activity but you are flexible enough to support your partner's willingness to do these things, with love. Because if the person you are with loves something, then perhaps you should look into it to see why there is so much love for that activity.

Hubie: Right.

Rose Trueheart: Okay, good. We are down to our last three questions and the one we have to go back to. What are the most important aspects of marriage? Before you said, that your marriage longevity happened because of love and communication. Are there any other specifics, maybe a few things that you think are the MOST important aspects?

Hubie: Honesty, open-mindedness and patience.

Rose Trueheart: Yes. Those are long-termers. Those essentially stand-alone unless you want to add anything to that but I think they are pretty clear. Do you think in terms of Black men as husbands and fathers, that their educational level matters relative to the educational status of the Black woman?

Hubie: That is a tough one. I would have to say, it really depends upon the two individuals. Because I know that I have heard stories of an educated women marrying a blue-collar worker and they are happier than most people who married someone who was essentially as educated as they were. I heard a story once. A gentleman said that his sister, who had the toughest time finding someone her "equal" educationally. She was highly educated. She finally started going out with somebody who was a blue-collar worker and she married the man. He said his sister was the happiest he is ever seen her. So, education, although it comes into play, I do not necessarily think that you have to marry someone that is on the same academic level as you. It is going to depend on the individuals and how much they are willing to learn and to accept? Am I making sense?

LONGEVITY

Rose Trueheart: I understand what you are saying. Now, in your situation in terms of your marriage, is their educational parity?

Hubie: We are the same now. Traci and I got married. Let me just back up for a second. When I came to Lemoyne College, I was 25 years old. I had been to college and dropped out. I first went to college when I was 17 years old. I was at SUNY Albany and I was so busy partying that I did not do too well. I dropped out. I actually went back to college when I was 24 and I picked up my Associate's degree. Then later, I got into Lemoyne College. I went there in December of 1979, I completed my studies. I got my Bachelor's and the rest is history.

Rose Trueheart: That is wonderful!

Hubie: Traci has her undergraduate degree from New York University. She has a Master's from Columbia University's Teacher's College. She has a School Administration Certificate from the College of Saint Rose. So, she did a little bit more academically than I did, but we both ended up with Bachelor's degrees and she has a Master's.

Rose Trueheart: That is cool. Okay, but that that was not a requirement in terms of your relationship. It is just the way it is. Would that be right?

Hubie: That is just the way it turned out. I had every intention of getting a degree. I should have gotten my college degree a year before she got hers. But I ended up dropping out of school. She encouraged me to go back and I eventually did and it all worked out.

Rose Trueheart: Well, that is great. That encouragement, is a big part, I believe, of marriage, too. I believe in encouraging each other. We are going to go back before we get to the last question. Did you have anything else you want to add to the question regarding educational level? Or, was that your full, complete answer?

Hubie: I think pretty much what I said, again, can go either way. For some people, they will not deal with anybody if they are not on their level, educationally. Others, are kind of open. And, you know, sometimes it works out when people are on two different levels and sometimes it does not. I do not think it is an absolute, but it tends to work better, I think, when people are on the same level.

Rose Trueheart: Okay. So, you added a little bit more there. So, you think it tends to work better? Can you just add a little clarity there? Why do you think it tends to work better?

Hubie: I think maturity plays a key role in it too. Education helps a person to grow. And if you do not have very much education, sometimes it is a little hard to grow.

Rose Trueheart: That is an important point. It makes sense. To get clarity, in terms of your two daughters, because when it is personal, it changes a little bit. Since education was very important for them, from your perspective, would you want them to be married to people who are educated, at least with a Bachelor's degree, higher education, given that they are both college graduates?

Hubie: : I would say yes.

Rose Trueheart: Please explain why.

A RETURN TO BLACK LOVE

Hubie: I cannot speak for them, but I have a feeling that they would want someone who has gone to college. Neither one of them are married at this point. But I have a feeling that they would want someone who has a college education.

Rose Trueheart: Now the question is, as their Father, is that what you believe? Because again, part of what I am trying to get at is as Black fathers, what are their wishes for their family and their children's experiences. Is that where you are as a Black Father? Is that what you would want for your daughters?

Hubie: That is what I would want for my daughters. But, ultimately, they are going to make the decision. My youngest daughter is dating a guy now. He is an Architect. My oldest daughter is not involved in a relationship right now. Her former boyfriend had a college degree. I think that they would seek out someone like that. They are not married, but if they decided that they wanted to do something else, and they truly loved the person and the person truly loved them, I would not put my two cents in.

234

LONGEVITY

Rose Trueheart: You clarified that completely so we will move on because I know the daughters do not want to be completely, 100%, or sometimes at all, influenced by their parents. But it is important, I believe, for us to understand as a collective, because often times it is felt that we, as Black people, do not have aspirations, particularly Black men, and I really want to find out from Black fathers, how do you feel about this? Do you think education is important? Do you think your lineage and history and all of those things are important? I am trying to dig in and get to those things to find out what matters, from the perspective of Black men. That takes us back to the question where you wanted a little more time and that is, do you think that history, lineage and legacy are important in terms of your family? I am asking you that for your perspective as a Black man, given the history that we have experienced in this society. As you know, many of our ancestors were slaves so since you grew up in this society, experiencing the United States of America, did you/do you find history, lineage and legacy important to you as a Black father and husband?

Hubie: I would have to say yes. Things that have been handed down to me in terms of work ethic, and perseverance--I think those things are very important. My hope is that I have pushed some of this down and it is embedded in my daughters.

Rose Trueheart: Did you share Black history with your children? As an example, we are getting ready to come upon Black History Month? Was that important or not important as your raised them?

Hubie: It was important. It still is important. When my kids went to nursery school, I sent them to a Black nursery school in Syracuse that was run by two of my friends, and it was very well run. They taught my kids Black history in preschool. They came home talking about Rosa Parks, Madam CJ. Walker, etc. So, Black history is very important to me. I do not know that I know enough of it. But, I do know the importance of it and that it matters.

Rose Trueheart: How much does legacy matter to you? Since you said it mattered for your life, for your family including your daughters and future grandchildren, does it fall into the category of importance for you, in terms of your family?

Hubie: Yes, it does.

Rose Trueheart: I would not presume that you would say no. But, it is important to ask because we have to think beyond us being here now and when we look at Black men in particular and Black families, legacy is not always a conversation that comes up. We see with other groups of people in society, that they prepare, or benefit from legacy, which was not possible for many Black people due to slavery. Now, we can think beyond the present. For example, purchasing of homes and passing them down to the family. Is that important from your vantage point?

Hubie: I think passing along property, wealth and knowledge are very important for the next generations.

Rose Trueheart: Ok! Excellent! My last question is do you have any parting thoughts about Black love and Black parenting, and any pearls of wisdom that you want to share? I know you have those pearls. You are not married for 39 years, and there are no pearls.

A RETURN TO BLACK LOVE

Hubie: You know, I was not always the man that I am now. I think my biggest problem, from years back, stemmed from my inability to communicate. I used to communicate, but it was not effective. What I have learned is that effective communication involves one person speaking, the other one listening, and then you reverse roles. That will help sustain your marriage.

Rose Trueheart: You started by responding about communication at the onset of this interview. So that is very important to you. My question had to do with Black love and Black parenting? I think that what you just said applies to both. Am I right about that?

Hubie: It applies to everyone. But it is coming from me. What you just heard came from a Black man. I am not saying it is unique to me and I agree, every relationship should involve listening and communicating. I do not know how to put it any better.

Rose Trueheart: You said that you are saying this as a Black man. Do you think this is something that needs to be reinforced and expressed specifically to Black men? Is

238

this something that you might feel is a shortcoming for Black men in general?

Hubie: I do not think it is a shortcoming across the board. But speaking for myself, it used to be. I think it would be beneficial if men, that knew this, would pass it on to their sons, or nephews, or any other Black men that are growing up who have to live in this world and eventually find himself a wife or girlfriend. It is a very important thing.

Rose Trueheart: Well, I think that is really outstanding and it is critical to hear that because it is important for us to share this information. I do not think society has collected enough words of wisdom and pearls of wisdom from Black men who have been in long term marriages with Black women. There is a tendency for us to hear a lot of negativity, but these pearls of wisdom and this understanding of how Black men are as fathers and husbands, although brief, and this understanding of what it means to be in a long term committed relationship is essential. Black love, and Black parenting is very important which is why I am so excited about this book.

A RETURN TO BLACK LOVE

Hubie: Well, I am sure when it is all done, it will be a great book.

Rose Trueheart: Thank you. Also, thank you so much for this interview!

Black Love Ingredients

There is a recipe for Black love, which entails commitment, communication, honesty, respect, trust, alignment and so many other key aspects that were discussed in the interviews throughout this book. However, recipes have key ingredients, which should be considered, with the opportunity to add and remove some of them to ensure that what you are trying to create, turns out just the way you want it. Below are some ingredients to consider. Perhaps a pinch of some, and a handful of others, stirred up together, will serve as your recipe of choice for Black Love.

Ingredients:

<u>Your Family</u>

Tell your Black family members, that you love, that you love them.

Love your children.

A RETURN TO BLACK LOVE

Hug your Black family members—your spouse, your children, your mother, your father and the rest of the crew.

Pick up your babies when they cry. Do not let them scream for you.

Read together.

Laugh together.

Cry together.

Make time for your family, no matter how busy you are.

Honor your parents.

Pray together.

Meditate together.

Think together.

Make education a top priority for your family.

Strive together for Black unity.

Know that Black is beautiful.

BLACK LOVE INGREDIENTS

Know that Black love IS the answer to our survival as Black people/families.

Yourself

Treat your body better than you treat your car. If you will not put unknown things (or what is not good for it) in your car, to make it run, have the same principle for your body.

Love your hair, as it grows from your scalp. It is your crown.

Moisturize your beautiful skin.

Take frequent naps.

Stand up for what you know, intuitively, is right.

Pray in conversation, rather than desperation.

Take long hot showers.

Soak in hot water, to soothe your bones.

Sit down, be quiet, listen and learn, when you do not know.

A RETURN TO BLACK LOVE

Do not be a bull in a China closet. Take your time adjusting to new people, spaces and places.

Soak in the sun.

Take your time with others.

Be patient.

Know your place at the table, in every situation.

Respect your elders.

Do not be afraid to ask for what you believe you are worth.

Do not laugh when something is not funny, just to please someone else.

Be and love yourself.

Live in the present understanding that tomorrow is not promised to you, but know that time is infinite.

Honor your faith.

Strive for peace.

BLACK LOVE INGREDIENTS

Love yourself just the way you are. Any improvements should be on your terms and nobody else's.

Be loyal to your friends but not to a fault.

If you have one good friend, you have more than your share.

Sleep when you need to or just because you want to.

Work to live. Do not live to work.

Think prosperously and avoid scarcity consciousness. There is more than enough for everyone.

Get out of your comfort zone.

Be a leader, not a follower.

Dance like nobody is watching, even when they are.

Consider others that matter to you, in your decision-making.

Listen to a variety of music.

If you are the only Black person in a place, or one of a few, walk as if you belong, because you do!

A RETURN TO BLACK LOVE

Sit quietly, alone and think, often.

Breathe, even when you feel you cannot.

Weep when you need to.

Travel, travel, travel!

Write letters to your loved ones, to tell them how you feel, even if you do not mail them.

Work hard and play harder.

Think.

Forgive.

Debate.

Be assertive when you need to be.

Be calm when you need to be.

Cook. It is the easiest way to be an alchemist.

Know that money is NOT the root of all evil but the love of it is.

Strive for abundance and prosperity.

BLACK LOVE INGREDIENTS

Exercise to keep your body fit and strong.

Drink plenty of water as a necessity, daily.

Spend time enjoying nature.

Have faith, not fear.

Smile.

Breathe.

Relax.

Your Food

Eat healthy with your family: (For example: organic fruits and vegetables, no hormones and antibiotics in your meat and poultry, grass fed beef, grass fed milk, brown rice, wheat and whole grain bread, etc.).

Modify your recipes, based on what works for you and your family, health-wise and economically.

Avoid white refined sugar and white bread—go for the brown—it is natural.

When entering a supermarket, start in the produce section and then seek other items.

A RETURN TO BLACK LOVE

Eat Slowly. Enjoy and savor every morsel of your food.

Eat to live, do not live to eat.

You do not have to "clean your plate," but avoid wasting food.

Avoid fast and processed food.

Indulge yourself with a delicious, at your favorite restaurant(s), whenever you can afford to, unashamedly.

Black Love Affirmations

I am Black and proud to be so.

I am rejoicing at the prospect that I, a Black person, have chosen to spend my life with a Black man or woman.

I am present for my children.

I am prosperous and abundant and deserve to be so.

I am an excellent communicator with my family and beyond.

I am happy with my hair the way it grows from my scalp.

I am happy with my Black skin.

I am happy that I respect my elders in every situation with them.

I am joyous that I have Black children to love and cherish.

I am a hugger and enjoy hugging Black people, especially my family members.

A RETURN TO BLACK LOVE

I am delighted that, as a Black person, I enjoy, love, date and want to marry/married a Black person.

I am a thinker and process information for myself.

I am a life-long learner and enjoy my history, as an African person in the U.S., as an American (or not).

I am strong and courageous in the face of adversity.

I am confident in my ability to succeed in a relationship with longevity being the goal.

I am releasing any negative familial energy through my breath.

I am relaxed.

I am faithful, not fearful.

I am a spiritual being having a human experience in a Black body.

I am living in the present because tomorrow is not promised to me, knowing that time is infinite.

I am free.

BLACK LOVE AFFIRMATIONS

I am compassionate.

I am merciful and forgiving.

I am trusting the process.

I am letting go of what is not mine.

I am a spirit unfolding.

I am comfortable laughing or crying when I need/want to.

I am unapologetically Black.

About the Author

DR. PATTI ROSE TRUEHEART acquired her B.A. from LeMoyne College, her M.P.H. from Yale University, followed by her Ed.D from Teachers College, Columbia University. She has taught full-time at the University of Miami, Florida International University and Nova Southeastern University. She has also taught as an Adjunct Professor at Florida Atlantic University, Springfield College, Worcester State College, and Barry University. In recent years, during many summers, she taught Chinese college students, as a Visiting Professor, at universities in Shanghai, Guangzhou, Shenzhen and Chengdu, China and at a University in Taiwan.

Rose Trueheart has given keynote addresses, conference presentations, and workshops at many national colleges and universities and other venues,

ABOUT THE AUTHOR

including Louisiana State University (LSU), Yale University, Teachers College, Columbia University, Le Moyne College, Ross University, Des Moines University Medical School, Miami Dade College, the American Public Health Association, and the National Association of Health Care Executives. Her international presentations have included conferences in Nairobi, Kenya; Barcelona, Spain; Paris, France and the islands of Aruba, St. Thomas, and Puerto Rico. Her current administrative role is Director and Founder of her own firm, Rose Consulting. Administratively, prior positions have included President and CEO and Vice President of Community Health Centers in New Jersey and Florida.

She has language skills in both Spanish and Mandarin through her travels and intensive study. Her passion is to travel the globe, having travelled to over 50 countries, to understand the world and to share her knowledge through her writing, teaching, and speaking engagements. Her cultural travel, work, and research have included journeys to Puerto Rico, Mexico, Fiji, Australia, New Zealand, Africa (Tanzania, Ghana, South Africa, Egypt, Kenya, Senegal, and the Cape Verde Islands), Europe (Greece, Belgium, Denmark, Germany, The United Kingdom, Ireland, Iceland, Monaco, Turkey, Spain, Italy, France, Portugal, and the Netherlands), the Caribbean (Jamaica, Tortola, St. Thomas, St. Lucia, Antigua, and Barbados), Latin, Central, and South America (Belize,

ABOUT THE AUTHOR

Cuba, Guatemala, Honduras, Nicaragua, Brazil, Costa Rica, Panama, and the Dominican Republic), and Asia, including, United Arab Emirates, India, Sri Lanka, Japan, South Korea, China, The Maldives, Vietnam, Singapore, Bali, and Thailand.

Dr. Rose Trueheart has been married for 36 years and is the mother of two.

Made in the USA
Columbia, SC
04 April 2022

58425102R00167